Forts and Battlefields

EXPLORE AMERICA

Forts and Battlefields

THE READER'S DIGEST ASSOCIATION, INC.
Pleasantville, New York / Montreal

Forts and Battlefields was created and produced by St. Remy Multimedia Inc.

Staff for Forts and Battlefields
Series Editor: Elizabeth Cameron
Art Director: Solange Laberge
Editor: Elizabeth Warrington Lewis
Assistant Editor: Neale McDevitt
Photo Researcher: Linda Castle
Cartography: Hélène Dion, David Widgington
Designer: Anne-Marie Lemay
Research Editor: Robert B. Ronald
Contributing Researcher: Olga Dzatko
Copy Editors: Joan Page McKenna, Judy Yelon
Index: Linda Cordella Cournoyer
System Coordinator: Éric Beaulieu
Technical Support: Mathieu Raymond-Beaubien,
Jean Sirois
Scanner Operators: Martin Francoeur, Sara Grynspan

St. Remy Staff
President, Chief Executive Officer: Fernand Lecoq
President, Chief Operating Officer: Pierre Léveillé
Vice President, Finance: Natalie Watanabe
Managing Editor: Carolyn Jackson
Managing Art Director: Diane Denoncourt
Production Manager: Michelle Turbide

Writers: Rod Gragg—Fort Laramie, Fort Sumter
Jim Henderson—Battle of New Orleans, Siege of Vicksburg
Bruce Heydt—War in Pennsylvania
Steven Krolak—Battle of the Little Bighorn, Pearl Harbor
Elizabeth Warrington Lewis—The French and Indian War
Margaret Locklair—Surrender at Yorktown
Kathryn Robinson—Forts of San Juan

Contributing Writers: Adriana Barton, Maxine Cuttler,
Katy McDevitt, Patricia McDevitt

Address any comments about *Forts and Battlefields*
to Editor, U.S. General Books, c/o Customer Service,
Reader's Digest, Pleasantville, NY 10570

Reader's Digest Staff
Editor: Kathryn Bonomi
Art Editor: Eleanor Kostyk
Production Supervisor: Mike Gallo
Editorial Assistant: Mary Jo McLean

Reader's Digest General Books
Editor-in-Chief, Books and Home
Entertainment: Barbara J. Morgan
Editor, U.S. General Books: David Palmer
Executive Editor: Gayla Visalli
Art Director: Joel Musler

Opening photographs
Cover: El Morro Fortress, Puerto Rico
Back Cover: Valley Forge National Historical Park,
Pennsylvania
Page 2: Chickamauga National Military Park, Georgia
Page 5: Little Bighorn National Monument, Montana

Library of Congress Cataloging in Publication Data

Forts & battlefields.
        p.   cm.—(Explore America)
     Includes index.
     ISBN 0-89577-963-3
     1. Fortification—United States—Guidebooks. 2. Battlefields—United
States—Guidebooks 3. United States—Guidebooks.
I. Series.
     E159.F695   1997
     917.304'929—dc21   97-2127

CONTENTS

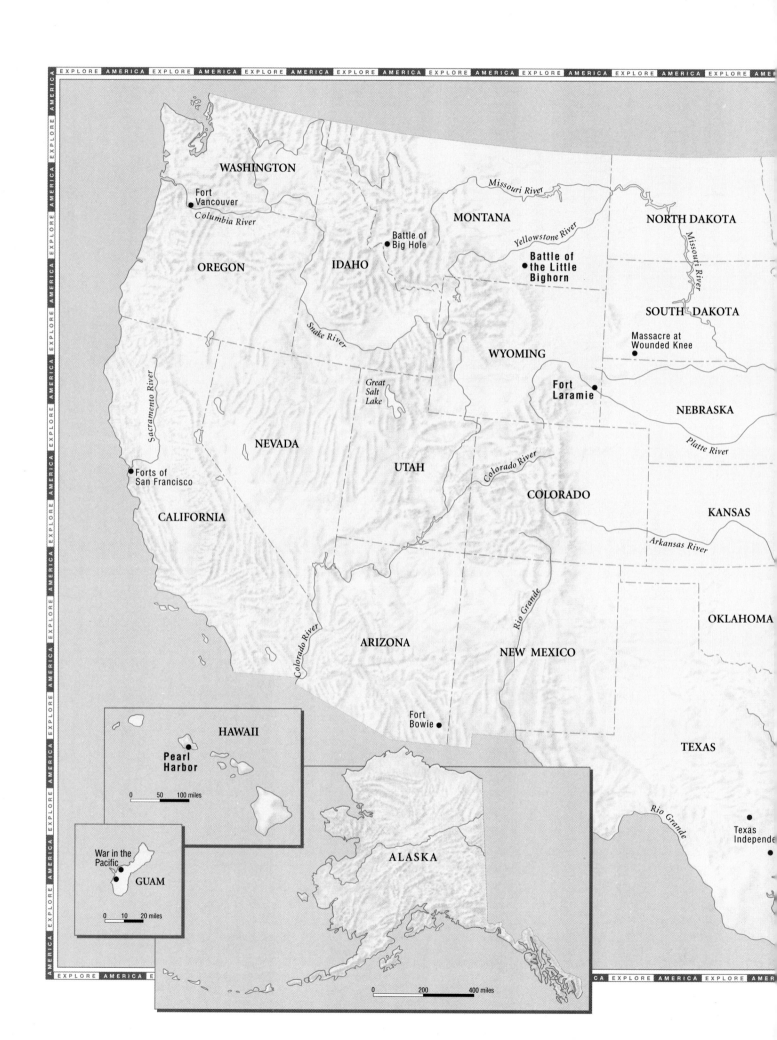

WASHINGTON

Fort
Vancouver

Columbia River

OREGON

Battle of
Big Hole

IDAHO

MONTANA

Missouri River

Yellowstone River

NORTH DAKOTA

**Battle of
the Little
Bighorn**

Missouri River

SOUTH DAKOTA

Snake River

WYOMING

Massacre at
Wounded Knee

Great
Salt
Lake

**Fort
Laramie**

Sacramento River

NEVADA

UTAH

Colorado River

NEBRASKA

Platte River

Forts of
San Francisco

CALIFORNIA

COLORADO

KANSAS

Arkansas River

Colorado River

ARIZONA

NEW MEXICO

Rio Grande

OKLAHOMA

Fort
Bowie

TEXAS

HAWAII

**Pearl
Harbor**

0   50   100 miles

Rio Grande

Texas
Independe

War in the
Pacific

GUAM

0   10   20 miles

ALASKA

0   200   400 miles

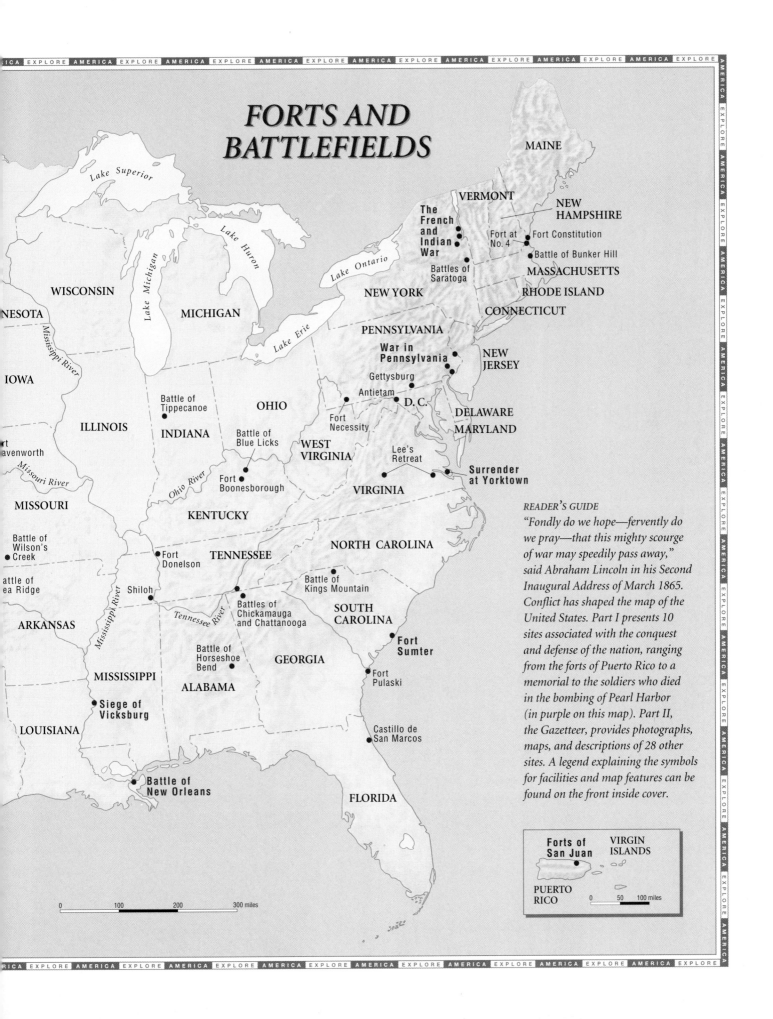

FORTS AND BATTLEFIELDS

READER'S GUIDE

"Fondly do we hope—fervently do we pray—that this mighty scourge of war may speedily pass away," said Abraham Lincoln in his Second Inaugural Address of March 1865. Conflict has shaped the map of the United States. Part I presents 10 sites associated with the conquest and defense of the nation, ranging from the forts of Puerto Rico to a memorial to the soldiers who died in the bombing of Pearl Harbor (in purple on this map). Part II, the Gazetteer, provides photographs, maps, and descriptions of 28 other sites. A legend explaining the symbols for facilities and map features can be found on the front inside cover.

FORTS OF SAN JUAN

Succumbing to neither war nor inclement weather, the forts of Old San Juan stand as proud testaments to the resilient defenses built in the New World colonies.

Vast open ground covers the northwesternmost promontory of Old San Juan, Puerto Rico's historic capital. Denuded of trees, baked by the tropical sun, and swept by westerly trade winds, the grassy field sprawls before an ancient fort. This open area, which was landscaped to leave enemy soldiers exposed to withering cannon fire, has now been taken over by visitors and local kite-fliers. In the distance sits a fortress known as El Morro, long and low and deceptively ordinary. A bridge crosses a dry moat to the entrance, where the walls reveal their monumental proportions. Beyond this threshold lies a courtyard bordered by a honeycomb network of vaulted rooms. On this ground, disciplined soldiers once practiced their drills.

Ramps lead to the highest of El Morro's six tiers, a hornwork, so named because its shape resembles a bull's horns. The five terraces below descend to the rough waters of the Atlantic. From this spectacular vantage point, it is apparent why El Morro has been called one of the most dramatic citadels ever built. El Morro, along with its sister fortress, San Cristóbal, and the walls that encircle the old city rank as marvels of military architectural design. Standing at the summit of El Morro, visitors gaze upon almost half a millennium of architecture: The hornwork was begun in the 16th century, expanded in the 18th century, and topped by a lighthouse in the 19th century and then an artillery observation post in the 20th century.

The main artillery ramp, a steep incline framed by narrow stairs, leads from the main plaza on level five to the Main Battery, a massive U-shaped structure holding the fort's largest concentration of cannons. Stairs descend to a lower patio on level three and vaulted rooms, known as casemates, surround the sand-packed patio. An inconspicuous passageway descends from the patio area to the oldest part of El Morro: a small, dimly lit tower room with a masonry floor and domed ceiling built in 1539. Burrowed in the brick walls is the scar of a shell fragment dating from the Spanish-American War. The steps once led to a water-level battery whose cannons pocked the hulls of enemy ships. Shadowed recesses mark windows, long since bricked over.

El Morro was not always the imposing structure that visitors see today, perched regally at the entrance to San Juan Bay. Its beginnings were humble. In 1508 the Spanish explorer Juan Ponce de León established Puerto Rico's first settlement some two miles south of the bay. But by 1521, the settlers had tired of defending the swampy, mosquito-infested village from the increasingly hostile local Taíno Indians and they moved to the breezy three-and-a-half-mile-long islet known today as Old San Juan.

Although Puerto Rico lay far away from the vast riches of the New World, its location at the gateway to the Indies was of great strategic importance to Spain. Pirates and Spain's enemies also coveted the small island, compelling the Spanish to fortify its Puerto Rican settlements.

San Juan's first fort was Casa Blanca, a small blockhouse built in 1523 and fortified in 1525. Several years later work began on a permanent

stronghold less than a half-mile from Casa Blanca. La Fortaleza, the Spanish word for "fortress," was positioned on the inland side of the islet, a location that was far from advantageous. "Only blind men could have chosen such a site for a fort," complained historical chronicler Gonzalo Fernández de Oviedo at the time, and La Fortaleza never distinguished itself in battle. By the end of the century, La Fortaleza had been converted to the governor's mansion, and it is the oldest governor's residence still in use in the Western Hemisphere.

Oviedo's choice for a new site was the headland at the harbor entrance, a lofty site 100 feet above the water known as *el morro*. A small battery was constructed at the foot of the cliffs where three low-level cannons could blast away at the waterlines of enemy vessels. San Juan had become a fortified settlement.

BOLSTERING THE DEFENSES Because San Juan was under constant threat of raids by Carib Indians and invasion by European fleets, King Philip II of Spain bolstered the settlement's defenses. San Juan was turned into a presidio housing a garrison of professional soldiers, and in 1589 El Morro

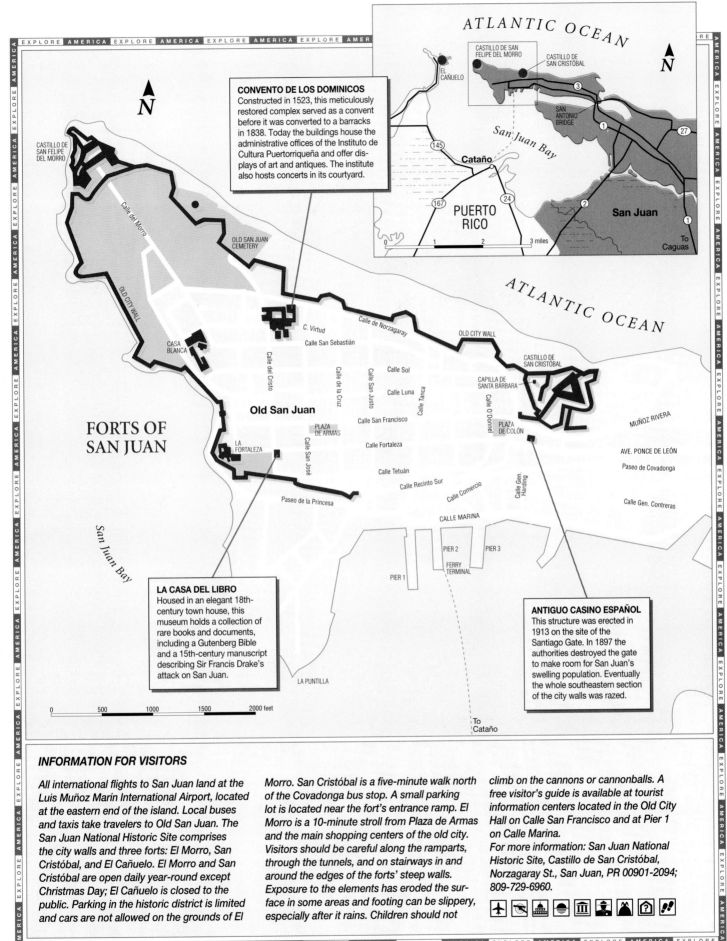

N

CONVENTO DE LOS DOMINICOS
Constructed in 1523, this meticulously restored complex served as a convent before it was converted to a barracks in 1838. Today the buildings house the administrative offices of the Instituto de Cultura Puertorriqueña and offer displays of art and antiques. The institute also hosts concerts in its courtyard.

ATLANTIC OCEAN

N

CASTILLO DE SAN FELIPE DEL MORRO

EL CAÑUELO

CASTILLO DE SAN FELIPE DEL MORRO

CASTILLO DE SAN CRISTÓBAL

San Juan Bay

SAN ANTONIO BRIDGE

145

3

1

27

Cataño

PUERTO RICO

167

24

San Juan

1

To Caguas

0   1   2   3 miles

CASTILLO DE SAN FELIPE DEL MORRO

Calle del Morro

OLD SAN JUAN CEMETERY

OLD CITY WALL

CASA BLANCA

ATLANTIC OCEAN

C. Virtud

Calle de Norzagaray

Calle San Sebastián

OLD CITY WALL

CASTILLO DE SAN CRISTÓBAL

Calle del Cristo

Calle de la Cruz

Calle San Justo

Calle Sol

Calle San Francisco

Calle Luna

Calle Tanca

CAPILLA DE SANTA BÁRBARA

Calle O'Donnel

MUÑOZ RIVERA

Old San Juan

PLAZA DE ARMAS

Calle San José

LA FORTALEZA

Calle Fortaleza

PLAZA DE COLÓN

AVE. PONCE DE LEÓN

Paseo de Covadonga

FORTS OF SAN JUAN

Calle Tetuán

Calle Recinto Sur

Calle Gen. Harding

Calle Gen. Contreras

Paseo de la Princesa

Calle Comercio

CALLE MARINA

San Juan Bay

PIER 2   PIER 3

FERRY TERMINAL

PIER 1

LA CASA DEL LIBRO
Housed in an elegant 18th-century town house, this museum holds a collection of rare books and documents, including a Gutenberg Bible and a 15th-century manuscript describing Sir Francis Drake's attack on San Juan.

LA PUNTILLA

ANTIGUO CASINO ESPAÑOL
This structure was erected in 1913 on the site of the Santiago Gate. In 1897 the authorities destroyed the gate to make room for San Juan's swelling population. Eventually the whole southeastern section of the city walls was razed.

To Cataño

0   500   1000   1500   2000 feet

INFORMATION FOR VISITORS

All international flights to San Juan land at the Luis Muñoz Marín International Airport, located at the eastern end of the island. Local buses and taxis take travelers to Old San Juan. The San Juan National Historic Site comprises the city walls and three forts: El Morro, San Cristóbal, and El Cañuelo. El Morro and San Cristóbal are open daily year-round except Christmas Day; El Cañuelo is closed to the public. Parking in the historic district is limited and cars are not allowed on the grounds of El

Morro. San Cristóbal is a five-minute walk north of the Covadonga bus stop. A small parking lot is located near the fort's entrance ramp. El Morro is a 10-minute stroll from Plaza de Armas and the main shopping centers of the old city. Visitors should be careful along the ramparts, through the tunnels, and on stairways in and around the edges of the forts' steep walls. Exposure to the elements has eroded the surface in some areas and footing can be slippery, especially after it rains. Children should not

climb on the cannons or cannonballs. A free visitor's guide is available at tourist information centers located in the Old City Hall on Calle San Francisco and at Pier 1 on Calle Marina.
For more information: San Juan National Historic Site, Castillo de San Cristóbal, Norzagaray St., San Juan, PR 00901-2094; 809-729-6960.

The solid walls of El Morro, opposite page, attest to the skill of the engineers who designed the fortress to withstand cannon blasts and violent tropical storms.

SOLDIERS' HOME
The graceful interior of the San Cristóbal barracks, right, makes it easy for visitors to forget the fort's deadly purpose. The barracks comprised eight vaulted rooms that could house more than 200 men.

was given its hornwork and the name Castillo de San Felipe del Morro. The impressive fort of today was beginning to take shape.

El Morro's first real test came in 1595, when the notorious British admiral Sir Francis Drake learned that a crippled Spanish galleon loaded with riches was moored in San Juan and he headed there with 27 ships, manned by 2,500 sailors. But Drake never made it into the harbor. Launching volley after

volley of lethal cannon fire, San Juan's defenders held the invading forces at bay. One report says that a cannonball ripped through Drake's cabin, splintering a stool from under him and killing two men. After several days marked by failed attempts to penetrate the Spanish defenses, Drake withdrew and sailed to Panama in search of easier prey.

The victory over Drake would come back to haunt the defenders of El Morro three years later. The British earl of Cumberland, learning from Drake's mistakes, realized that San Juan could not be taken by water. He bypassed the harbor and anchored his fleet of 21 ships east of San Juan islet. After he had established a beachhead, Cumberland made his way to San Antonio Bridge, the only land access to San Juan. A small band of Spanish sol-

diers valiantly fought off the 1,700-man English army for two hours—Cumberland himself almost drowned when he fell into the water in heavy armor—but the Spanish were forced to retreat.

At daybreak on June 18, 1598, British soldiers marched into San Juan. The town was deserted, most of its inhabitants having retreated to the mainland or to El Morro. The British cut off supply lines to the fort and bombarded it from a distance, then sat back and waited for a signal of surrender. On July 1 Spanish soldiers marched out of the fort carrying white flags. Puerto Rico had become an English colony. But British rule did not last long. The occupying soldiers had survived Spanish bullets and cannonballs, only to succumb to a more ruthless foe—nature. The tropical summer heat made food supplies susceptible to contamination, and the resulting dysentery killed 400 soldiers and another 400 fell ill. Cumberland, no longer able to control the town, sent his men in retreat, burning and looting as they marched away.

The Spanish returned to San Juan after several months and set about improving their defenses.

REMNANTS OF A VIOLENT PAST
Made to inflict the greatest degree of damage on enemy ships, the authentic 16-pound cannonballs, above, stacked in a pyramid at San Cristóbal, could hit targets up to a mile away.

They built a small wooden fort on El Cañuelo Island (now Cabras Island), on the western side of the bay, and heightened the walls of El Morro. The new fortifications passed the next test with mixed results. In 1625 Boudewijn Hendricksz and his fleet of 17 Dutch ships lay siege to San Juan. Sailing into the teeth of El Morro's cannons, the Dutch gained entrance to the harbor. San Juan's population fled once again, but this time El Morro and its defenders were able to withstand the siege. After 21 days of battle, the Dutch were forced to withdraw when the defenders of the fort successfully repelled their fleet with cannon fire. The invaders burned San Juan to the ground as they left.

The Spanish raised their town from the smoldering ruins and began work on new and improved fortifications. By the middle of the 17th century, they had constructed a small fort at San Cristóbal and erected walls around the town on all but the northern side. The city could be entered by way of only three gates, which were locked at night.

IRISH CONNECTION In the mid-1700's the new Spanish monarch, Charles III, assigned Irishman Alexander O'Reilly—who had joined the Spanish army in his youth and later served as the governor of Madrid—to the task of converting San Juan into a defense of the first order. O'Reilly stepped up discipline, rooted out corrupt officers, and reorganized the militia. And he and his chief military engineer, Thomas O'Daly, developed plans to beef up the military fortifications.

For a quarter of a century O'Daly and his collaborator, Juan Francisco Mestre, shored up the defenses. The Main Battery at El Morro was enlarged, the hornwork redesigned, and a wall was built that unified the lower and upper halves of the fort. The city walls were strengthened, and a section was added to the northern coast, thus completely enclosing the city. The eastern edge of the islet got first and second lines of defense, and the site's existing forts were modernized. Today about three miles of walls, some measuring 60 feet high and 16 feet thick at the top, wrap around much of the old city, making these the best surviving examples of Spanish city walls in the New World.

The most spectacular work took place at San Cristóbal. Unlike other coastal forts, San Cristóbal was designed primarily for defense against land attack. Hundreds of day laborers, convicts, soldiers, and slaves worked to strengthen the fort. They used native timber for everything from pegs to rafters and made a cementlike material, known as *mampostería,* from limestone, sandstone, and clays. Rope and metalware were imported from Spain, and stone was mined from local quarries.

When visitors enter Castillo de San Cristóbal they see a fort that looks much as it did in the late 1700's. This is the largest fortification that was ever built by the Spaniards in the Americas. Today it sprawls over some 18 acres, but it was at least one-third larger up until the end of the past century, when parts of the fort and the city walls were knocked down to accommodate a swelling population. A walkway goes up to the entrance of the fort and a large triangular parade ground, where soldiers were drilled relentlessly.

From the Main Battery on the second level, the sheer ingenuity of the engineering work becomes apparent. The land approach to San Juan was protected by a triangular outworks made up of a maze of small forts, moats, tunnels, gunpowder magazines, trenches, and mining galleries extending in ever-higher levels to the main fort. Even the largest army would be hard-pressed to overrun this complex series of fortifications quickly. If the enemy overtook one section of the outworks, the defenders could stop them in their tracks by blowing up the nearest passageway.

Vaulted casemates held the kitchen, latrines, sleeping quarters, and storage rooms. In times of battle, artillerymen prayed to their patron saint, Santa Bárbara, in the fort's chapel. Eight large rooms housed up to 212 soldiers. During a battle, however, when six soldiers were needed to man each of the more than 450 cannons mounted at the fort, the overflow troops were lodged in town. One refurbished barrack room contains several long platforms that could sleep 28 men at a time. Overhead shelves with pegs were used for storage. Visitors see wooden tables set for a meal and a domino game halted in progress.

The officers' barracks stand behind two circular drainage wells that shielded the water supply from enemy fire. Four large underground cisterns stored more than 700,000 gallons of rainwater, which was channeled from the upper levels. Water was such a precious commodity that soldiers were forbidden to allow animals near it—even to move the cannons that weighed up to five tons along the ramps—for fear that animal droppings might contaminate the water supply.

Cannons were pointed toward the ocean along the North Battery and the northern side of the Main Battery. From the North Battery visitors can look down at the Devil's Sentry Box, an eerie looking tower at the water's edge. It is one of numerous small watchtowers built on the outer corners of bastions and along the city walls. The night sentries would keep each other awake by shouting

DEADLY FIELD OF FIRE
Visitors who climb up to El Morro's lighthouse are afforded spectacular views of the area south of the fort, below. In the 16th century the wide field, or glacis, was denuded, smoothed over, and sloped up toward the fort so that approaching enemy troops were left entirely exposed to lethal cannon blasts.

"*Alerta!*" The Devil's Sentry Box received its name because one night, centuries ago, a sentry failed to respond to the "*alerta*" cry. He was never seen again. Rumor has it that the devil hustled him away.

COLLAPSE OF AN EMPIRE

On April 17, 1797, the British fleet, commanded by Sir Ralph Abercromby, anchored off the coast east of San Juan. Some 3,000 troops marched ashore the next day and prepared to attack. Supported by long-range cannon fire from San Cristóbal a mile away, the Spanish artillery crews manning forts along the first and second lines of defense wreaked havoc on the English lines; after 17 days the British sailed away in defeat. Abercromby wrote that San Juan could have resisted 10 times more firepower.

The San Juan forts could not hold out against the U.S. Navy. During the 1898 Spanish-American War, American armored battleships bombarded the city, damaging several fort walls, the lighthouse, and buildings in the old section. When America won the war, Cuba gained sovereignty; Puerto Rico, Guam, and the Philippines were turned over to the United States; and Spain lost the New World empire it had struggled to hold on to for 400 years.

Never again were the forts attacked. During the first half of the 20th century, the fortifications belonged to the U.S. Army, which modernized the bunkers and batteries and added concrete observation posts and communication centers against the threat of German submarines during World War II. The field in front of El Morro was used for everything from an army golf course to officers' housing. In 1949 El Morro, San Cristóbal, El Cañuelo, and the city walls were designated a National Historic Site and 20th-century additions were eliminated for historical authenticity.

But for an occasional costumed interpreter, the forts are left to tell their own tale. Visitors stand on the bastions, gazing out to sea, and slip back in time to an age when vision and determination, wealth and toil created monuments that helped shape the history of the New World.

NEARBY SITES & ATTRACTIONS

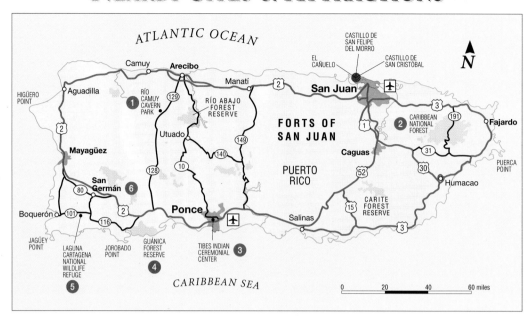

1 RÍO CAMUY CAVERN PARK

Established in 1976, this 300-acre park contains numerous caves, canyons, and sinkholes, and the world's third-largest subterranean river. A slide show detailing the geological history of the caves is presented at the park's visitor center, where a tram departs for the entrance of the cave. From there, guides lead visitors on a series of walkways through the winding cave system. Footpaths link the park's massive sinkholes, including 400-foot-deep Tres Pueblos Sinkhole. After descending 205 steps into Spiral Sinkhole, visitors come to Spiral Cave. In 1984 archeologists discovered shells and shaped rocks in the sinkhole, evidence that the cave was used by pre-Columbian Taíno Indians. The park also offers picnic sites and nature trails. Located 20 miles south of Arecibo on Hwy. 129.

2 CARIBBEAN NATIONAL FOREST

These 27,846 acres constitute the only tropical forest in the U.S. national forest system and the largest tract of woodland in Puerto Rico. The rain forest has been protected since 1876 when, under Spanish rule, it was designated as a Crown forest. In 1903 Pres. Theodore Roosevelt named the area the Luquillo Forest Reserve. In 1917 the U.S. Forest Service added more land to the reserve, and in 1935 the Luquillo Forest Reserve's name was changed to the Caribbean National Forest. Most locals disregard the official names and refer to the region simply as El Yunque, for the 3,500-foot-tall peak that juts from the coastal plain. Encompassing four separate forest zones and fed by an annual rainfall of 100 billion gallons, the national forest supports some 250 species of trees, only 6 of which are found in the continental United States. The white-barked tabonuco tree is the dominant species in the tabonuco forest, found in the region's lower slopes. Above the 2,000-foot level, visitors can walk among colorado trees that are thousands of years old. One specimen, estimated to be 2,500 years old, has a trunk that measures more than 23 feet in circumference. Within the lush palm forest, sierra palms tower above mosses, ferns, yagrumos, and other indigenous plants. The dwarf forest, located at the Caribbean National Forest's highest elevations, is populated by trees no more than 12 feet tall. The national forest is dissected by more than 50 miles of hiking trails, some of which wind along mountain slopes. Primary trails include El Yunque, El Toro, Mount Britton, and Big Tree. The El Toro and El Yunque trails lead to the summits of the forest's two highest peaks. The region's wildlife includes the endangered red, green, and blue Puerto Rican parrot, scaly-naped pigeon, Puerto Rican tanager, bare-legged owl, and quail dove. The forest surrounds the headwaters of eight major rivers that support an abundance of crayfish and shrimp. Located 35 miles southeast of San Juan on Hwy. 191.

At the Tibes Indian Ceremonial Center, visitors can see several bateyes, below, areas encircled by riverbed stones and used for ceremonies and ball games. Some of the stones are etched with petroglyphs that are thousands of years old.

3 TIBES INDIAN CEREMONIAL CENTER

Located on the site of three successive native cultures, the center contains nine dance grounds, a museum, and a reconstructed Taíno Indian village featuring reed-roofed structures. The area was first occupied from A.D. 300 to 600, the latter part of the Igneri period. Anthropologists have identified axes, ceramic vessels, and amulets from this time, along with one of the Caribbean's oldest cemeteries, where more than 180 graves have been found. The people who inhabited the site during the pre-Taíno period, from A.D. 600 to 1100, left behind adzes, frog-shaped amulets, and numerous petroglyphs. Visitors to the center can explore 10 restored *bateyes,* used for a variety of tribal activities, such as ceremonial dances and a game similar to soccer. The rectangular courts at the center range in size: the largest one measures 215 by 45 feet. Within one *bateye* are stones that align with the sun during solstices and equinoxes. A museum displays artifacts found at the site. Located in Ponce on Hwy. 2.

4 GUÁNICA FOREST RESERVE

Located on the southern coast of the island, the largest cactus scrub tropical forest in the world was designated an International Man and Biosphere Reserve by the United Nations in 1975. Visitors can explore most of the reserve's 1,620 acres on 36 miles of roads and trails that crisscross the landscape. More than 40 species of birds can be seen within the reserve's protective boundaries, including the Puerto Rican whippoorwill, a bird found nowhere else on the island. Bird-watchers also delight in spotting the orange-cheeked waxbill, Puerto Rican nightjar, and Puerto Rican bullfinch. The area's beautiful sandy beaches are home to several species of reptile, among which the *Ameiva wetmorei* lizard and

leatherback turtles are quite commonly seen. Mongooses can sometimes be observed prowling along the beach in search of the caches of green turtle eggs buried in the sand. There are more than 700 species of trees and plants within the forest reserve, including 48 rare species. Sparse rainfall and salt spray on the coast have created a perfect environment for sea grapes, milkweed, and buttonwood mangroves. Located 43 miles west of Ponce off Hwy. 116.

5 LAGUNA CARTAGENA NATIONAL WILDLIFE REFUGE

This refuge, centered on the largest remaining freshwater marsh in the Lajas Valley, provides a habitat for resident and migratory birds. Although a large portion of the 1,036-acre refuge is a lagoon, the rest of the territory encompasses wetland vegetation, abandoned pastureland, old sugar fields, and more than 250 acres of foothills of the Sierra Bermeja mountain range. Approximately 163 bird species can be sighted within the refuge, including the endangered Puerto Rican nightjar. Located 10 miles south of San Germán off Hwy. 101.

6 SAN GERMÁN

Founded in 1573, San Germán is known for its Colonial architecture. One of the town's most prominent Mediterranean-style structures is the Museo Porta Coeli. Built as a convent in 1606, it now serves as a museum for the display of religious art, including choral books and sculptures. The Old Municipal Building, built between 1839 and 1844, served as a prison until 1950 and has been restored to its 19th-century appearance. Most of the city's historic architectural sites are found in the Martin Quinones Plaza and the Parque de Santo Domingo, in the city center. Located on Hwy. 80 west of Ponce.

The cobblestone streets and brick sidewalks of San Germán add charm and style to the town's 19th-century houses, including Calle José Julian Acosta, left.

La Coca Falls, below, on the Quebrada La Coca River, lies within the Caribbean National Forest.

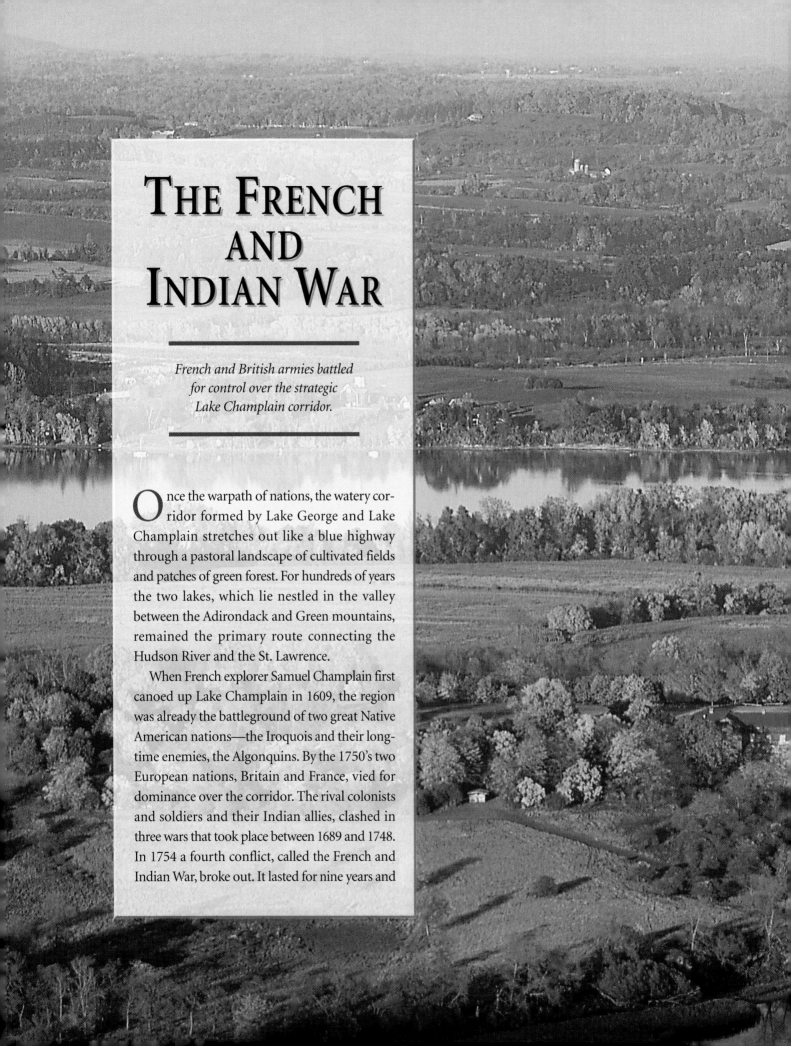

THE FRENCH AND INDIAN WAR

*French and British armies battled
for control over the strategic
Lake Champlain corridor.*

Once the warpath of nations, the watery corridor formed by Lake George and Lake Champlain stretches out like a blue highway through a pastoral landscape of cultivated fields and patches of green forest. For hundreds of years the two lakes, which lie nestled in the valley between the Adirondack and Green mountains, remained the primary route connecting the Hudson River and the St. Lawrence.

When French explorer Samuel Champlain first canoed up Lake Champlain in 1609, the region was already the battleground of two great Native American nations—the Iroquois and their long-time enemies, the Algonquins. By the 1750's two European nations, Britain and France, vied for dominance over the corridor. The rival colonists and soldiers and their Indian allies, clashed in three wars that took place between 1689 and 1748. In 1754 a fourth conflict, called the French and Indian War, broke out. It lasted for nine years and

SCENIC CRUISE
The steamboat Mohican, above, plies the blue waters of Lake George off Fort William Henry. Several companies offer excursions along the waterway, departing from the villages of Lake George, Larrabees Point, Ticonderoga, and other sites on the two lakes.

WHERE TWO WATERS MEET
Overleaf: Fort Ticonderoga, named after the Mohawk word meaning "Place Where Two Waters Meet," stands center stage where the La Chute River flows into Lake Champlain. When the French began construction on a fort at this critical portage in 1755, they named it Fort Vaudreuil, but it was known popularly as Carillon, a corruption of Carrion, after Philippe de Carrion, a Spanish fur trader whose post occupied the site in the 1670's.

when it was over the victorious British had chased the French from their positions along Lake Champlain and had seized control of all North America east of the Mississippi.

STRATEGIC SITE

Mount Defiance provides visitors with a panoramic view of Lake Champlain where it narrows at Fort Ticonderoga, an 18th-century fortress built by the French during the French and Indian War to command this section of the corridor. Not only did the fort overlook the lake, it also defended the critical portage linking Lake George with Lake Champlain, which was located in the dense woodland just south of the fort. Fur traders, war parties, and armies passed by the fort as they traveled between the English colonies in the south and New France in the north.

On a clear day, travelers looking north from Mount Defiance can see the steel form of the Lake Champlain Bridge, which connects Vermont to New York State. At the Crown Point State Historic Site, found at the New York entrance to the bridge, lie the ruins of two 18th-century edifices: a British fort, known as His Majesty's Fort of Crown Point, and a French fort, called St. Frédéric.

It was primarily from Fort St. Frédéric, named for Jean-Frédéric Phélypeaux de Maurepas, France's minister of the Department of the Marine, that France dominated the Lake Champlain region during the years leading up to the French and Indian War. The fort, erected between 1734 and 1737, consisted of a stone citadel four stories high, surrounded by masonry walls. The fortification was

INFORMATION FOR VISITORS

To reach Lake George Battlefield Park and Fort William Henry from Albany, NY, take I-87 to Exit 21 and then travel along Hwy. 9. For Fort Ticonderoga, take Exit 28 and then Hwy. 74. To reach the Crown Point State Historic Site, take Exit 28 off I-87 then take Hwy. 9N. The historic site is located near the Lake Champlain Bridge, four miles east of Hwys. 9N and 22. From Burlington, VT, take Hwy. 7, Hwy 22A, and Hwy. 17 south to the Lake Champlain Bridge at Chimney Point. All of the sites are open daily from mid-May until mid-October.
For more information: Lake Placid/Essex County Visitors Bureau, Box 220, RR 1, Bridge Rd., Crown Point, NY 12928; 518-597-4646.

HIGHLANDER'S GRAVE
The highlander Duncan Campbell, who was mortally wounded in the 1758 battle at Carillon, was buried in Fort Edward's Union Cemetery, below. Robert Louis Stevenson's poem, "Ticonderoga: A Legend of the West Highlands," recounts how Campbell was haunted by premonitions of dying "at the place with the awful name, Ticonderoga, the utterance of the dead."

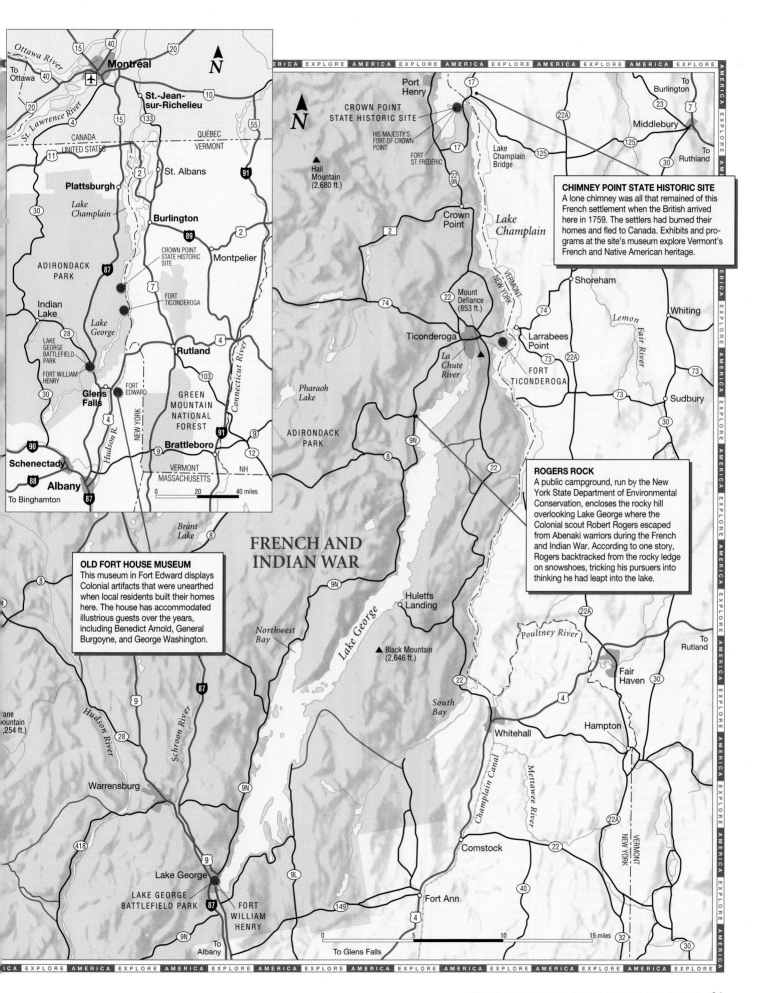

FRENCH AND INDIAN WAR

CHIMNEY POINT STATE HISTORIC SITE
A lone chimney was all that remained of this French settlement when the British arrived here in 1759. The settlers had burned their homes and fled to Canada. Exhibits and programs at the site's museum explore Vermont's French and Native American heritage.

ROGERS ROCK
A public campground, run by the New York State Department of Environmental Conservation, encloses the rocky hill overlooking Lake George where the Colonial scout Robert Rogers escaped from Abenaki warriors during the French and Indian War. According to one story, Rogers backtracked from the rocky ledge on snowshoes, tricking his pursuers into thinking he had leapt into the lake.

OLD FORT HOUSE MUSEUM
This museum in Fort Edward displays Colonial artifacts that were unearthed when local residents built their homes here. The house has accommodated illustrious guests over the years, including Benedict Arnold, General Burgoyne, and George Washington.

FRENCH POSSESSION
The white flag of the French Department of the Marine, above, which administered the forts of New France, waves in the wind above the stone foundations of Fort St. Frédéric at the Crown Point State Historic Site.

INDISPENSABLE ITEM
The powder horn of Peter Hart, below, a colonial in the British army who fought in the 1758 battle for Carillon, is on display at Fort Ticonderoga.

the first substantial one to be built in the Champlain Valley, and it contrasted with the wooden frontier defenses built by the British during the same period. To create this medieval-looking fortress, French Canadian builders boated down the waterway from Montreal bearing cargoes of hardware and ironwork, then quarried gray limestone on Isle La Motte and cut and shaped it on the site.

The foundations of the walls and the citadel are seen on the grassy bluff at the water's edge. In summer, dandelions run riot in the thick grass and wild yellow snapdragons cluster by the crumbling stone walls. Besides wandering through the ruins, visitors can picnic above the shoreline or inspect the old maps, drawings, weapons, and other artifacts that are on display in the visitor center at the Crown Point State Historic Site, which also offers a short film on the history of the site.

On his way to Canada in the summer of 1749, Swedish naturalist Pehr Kalm took shelter in the fort. He described the original structure in his journal: "On the eastern part of the fort is a high tower, which is proof against bombshells, provided with very thick and substantial walls, and well stored with cannon from the bottom almost to the very top." Kalm was welcomed

by the urbane and hospitable governor of the fort, Paul-Louis Dazemard de Lusignan, who "heaped kindness" on him and then sent him on his way, stocked with provisions for his journey. During his stay at the fort, Kalm heard several "bloodcurdling" shouts coming from the south—a vivid reminder that even in the years before the outbreak of the French and Indian War, Fort St. Frédéric was the staging place for raids by Canadians, Indians, and French. These raiding parties would leave the safety of the fort's walls and terrorize English settlers who were living unprotected along the frontiers of New York, New Hampshire, Massachusetts, and Connecticut.

Another fort visitor was Susannah Johnson who, along with her husband, three children, and several friends, was kidnapped by the Abenaki from the Johnson farmstead outside Charlestown, New Hampshire, during the summer of 1754. The Indians set off for Montreal to sell the settlers as slaves to the French and Canadians in the well-established traffic in Colonial captives. In an account published in 1841 Susannah described the harrowing journey. En route she went into labor and the Indians "shewed some humanity" and built a makeshift shelter for her by a brook. "About 10 o'clock a daughter was born. . . . My master looked into the booth, and clapped his hands with joy, crying two monies for me, two monies for me." Susannah named her daughter Captive.

When the group stopped at Fort St. Frédéric, the Indians celebrated the success of their raid by dancing outside the walls. Governor Lusignan invited Susannah and her fellow captives into the fort where they were offered food and fresh clothes. Following a four-day respite, they were returned to their Abenaki captors. Although Susannah spent three years in captivity, she bore no animosity toward the Indians, who she said treated her as well as any "civilized conquerors" would have done.

ORIGINS OF WAR The thriving traffic in captives fueled the hostilities between the British colonies and New France. By the mid-1750's, tensions were on the verge of exploding. With a burgeoning population of 1 million colonists, the British expanded their territory into the great valley of the Ohio River, an area the French claimed for themselves. The French built forts to defend their lands and the English responded in kind. In 1754 approximately 150 Virginia militiamen under Lieut. Col. George Washington fought a pitched battle with some 700 French and Indians at a crude stockade called Fort Necessity, near Uniontown, Pennsylvania. A third of Washington's men were killed in the fighting. When the Americans ran short of ammunition, Washington surrendered. The French and Indian War had commenced.

War erupted in the Lake Champlain region the following August when Indian agent William Johnson assembled an army of 1,500 British troops and some 40 Mohawk allies and led them to the southern end of Lac St. Sacrement, which Johnson

A GLANCE BACKWARD
An interpreter in an 18th-century French military uniform plays the bagpipes, left, in Fort Ticonderoga's Place of Arms, where French, then British, and later American soldiers once practiced their drills.

IN SAFE HANDS
The main museum building at Fort William Henry, below, displays an extensive collection of Colonial and Indian artifacts as well as life-size mannequins, created by cartoonist Jack Binder, that are posed in period settings to evoke the daily life of the garrison soldiers.

STRENGTH IN ALLIES

*A monument to William Johnson
and his Mohawk ally, King
Hendrick, right, stands in Lake
George Battlefield Park. It com-
memorates the victory of British
Colonial forces over the French
at the 1755 Battle of Lake George.
King Hendrick, who had reportedly
advised Johnson not to split his
army before the battle, is shown
handing the British commander
a bunch of arrows, a symbol of
strength in numbers.*

STRENGTH IN ALLIES
*A monument to William Johnson
and his Mohawk ally, King
Hendrick, right, stands in Lake
George Battlefield Park. It com-
memorates the victory of British
Colonial forces over the French
at the 1755 Battle of Lake George.
King Hendrick, who had reportedly
advised Johnson not to split his
army before the battle, is shown
handing the British commander
a bunch of arrows, a symbol of
strength in numbers.*

LIVING HISTORY
*Interpreters dressed as regimental
musicians of the 1st New York
Continental Line during the
American Revolution stroll the
ramparts of Fort Ticonderoga,
below. To distinguish themselves
from soldiers on the battlefield,
musicians typically wore uniforms
with the regimental colors reversed.
In this case, the 1st New York's traditional blue uniforms, faced with
red, have been reversed.*

promptly renamed Lake George after King George
II. After securing the lake, Johnson planned to
advance northward and oust the French from Fort
St. Frédéric, and thus from Lake Champlain.

The commander of the French forces at St.
Frédéric was the wily general Baron von Dieskau.
Hoping to halt the British in their tracks, he head-

ed north on Lake Champlain by bateaux and canoes
with 500 French regulars, 1,600 Canadians, and
700 Indians, and then portaged over to Lake
George. There, the French encountered Johnson's
troops, who had barricaded themselves behind
wagons, tree trunks, and bateaux on a ridge bor-
dering the lake. Against all odds, Johnson's forces
won the day-long clash. The battle is commemorated at the Lake George Battlefield Park in the
town of Lake George. Several memorials honor the
region's past, including one dedicated to four
unknown soldiers, who are believed to have been
killed in an ambush just before the fighting began.

FORT WILLIAM HENRY

About a quarter-mile from the
park on a wooden palisaded
structure on a 50-foot bluff
overlooking Lake George lies
the reconstruction of Fort
William Henry. Johnson's men started to build the
fort after their victory at the Battle of Lake George.
By the time the French tried again to expel the
British in 1757, the fort's four corner bastions, connected by stout wooden cribwork filled with earth,
were firmly implanted in the soil.

Visitors to Fort William Henry can tour the
museum, soldiers' barracks, powder magazine, and
the dungeon with its narrow cells. On the fort's
ramparts, costumed interpreters fire off a six-
pounder cannon and demonstrate the Brown Bess,
or tower musket, which was used by British soldiers during the 18th century.

On a midsummer day in 1757, soldiers manning
the fort's northern ramparts looked out and saw
a massive regatta of bateaux and war canoes heading down the lake toward them. This French army
of some 8,000 men included 1,800 Indians—1,000
from the *pays d'en haut* in the region of the upper
Great Lakes, as well as 800 mission Indians accompanied by their priests. The troops landed on the
western shore of Lake George and quickly set to
work building the trenches and breastworks necessary to stage a siege.

The French commander was the clever and ener-
getic Marquis Louis Joseph de Montcalm-Gozon de
Saint-Véran, invigorated by his brilliant victory at
Fort Oswego on Lake Ontario the year before.
Lieutenant Colonel George Monro, a Scottish veteran of the 35th Regiment, was in charge of the
defenders of Fort William Henry, an army of about
450 men. Another 2,500 of his men had taken positions in an entrenched camp almost a mile away.

The French didn't waste much time before they
called the English to surrender and sent in a red
flag of truce (white being the color of their ensign).
But Monro, who expected reinforcements from
Fort Edward, refused to give up. For three days

French mortars tossed 200-pound bombs at the fort. The fort's heavy guns and mortars began to crack under the strain of firing back. The men in the entrenched camp were convinced it was too risky to go up against Montcalm's vast army. Only a powerful sortie or a fresh supply of artillery could save the day. But the reinforcements never arrived and the British finally gave up.

To the outrage of his Indian allies, Montcalm gave the defeated army generous terms of surrender, allowing them to withdraw with the "honors of war." The British, in turn, promised not to bear arms against the French for 18 months.

As the withdrawing British hiked down the 15-mile road to Fort Edward, some of the Indians from Montcalm's army ambushed them. Stealing their belongings and slaughtering anyone who tried to resist or run away, the warriors took more than 500 captives, many of them women and children. James Fenimore Cooper dramatized these events in his 1826 novel, *The Last of the Mohicans*, which dwells on the savagery of the Indians. According to a 1990 historical account of the events by Ian K. Steele, however, the Indians had "spent weeks canoeing a thousand miles to fight for the martial trophies that were their only pay, were passports to manhood for some, and assurances of higher esteem for others." When they were betrayed by a conspiracy to defraud them of their promised share of the plunder, they attacked the British.

Montcalm ordered that Fort William Henry be burned to the ground, and led his army back to its position earlier in the summer—the French fort on the Ticonderoga peninsula, known as Carillon. At that time the peninsula was largely cleared of trees and looked little like the lovely wooded park that surrounds the reconstructed fort today. The soldiers cut firewood for the coming winter before most of them headed home to Canada to help bring in the harvest.

JUBILANT VICTORS
A 1930 watercolor by Harry Ogden, above, depicts the Marquis de Montcalm congratulating his troops at the Battle of Carillon on July 8, 1758. The painting is on display in the museum at Fort Ticonderoga.

Carillon is now known as Fort Ticonderoga. Costumed interpreters play the roles of soldiers garrisoned at the fort during the 18th and 19th centuries. The museum's collection of artifacts from the French and Indian War, the largest of its type in the northeast, includes weapons, paintings, and rare documents. Also on display is the silk suit worn by the fort's Canadian architect, Michel Chartier, Marquis de Lotbinière.

De Lotbinière began work on the new fort in 1755. By 1758, the summer after the French victory at Fort William Henry, Carillon was completed. Now the British forces would face an additional obstacle when they next tried to chase the French from Fort St. Frédéric.

This time the command of the British army was held by Maj. Gen. James Abercrombie, a man

trees to make a lethal abatis that stretched out in front of the wall for a distance of 100 yards.

In the early afternoon of July 8 the British infantry charged Montcalm's great log wall. As they stumbled over the pointed branches of the abatis, the French mowed them down with muskets fired through loopholes pierced in the wall. Again and again during the next six hours, Abercrombie, safe behind the British line, ordered his men to charge. In the early evening, Abercrombie acknowledged the futility of the attack and ordered a halt. Some 1,600 British soldiers were killed or wounded, among them 499 Black Watch highlanders—approximately half the regiment. An orderly retreat disintegrated into a mad dash for safety, as soldiers ran for their boats and rowed up the lake.

Visitors can walk through the woods that now cover much of the Carillon Battlefield within the

SOLDIERS' QUARTERS
The stone barracks at Fort Ticonderoga, right, were designed to sleep about 400 French soldiers. During the 1758 summer campaign, when the French army swelled into the thousands, the soldiers were quartered sous toile *(under canvas tents).*

described by his predecessor, Lord Loudoun, as "a very good Second Man anywhere."

In July 1758 Abercrombie advanced on Carillon with almost 16,000 men, outnumbering the French by five to one. But the French enjoyed one overwhelming advantage: the military genius of Marquis de Montcalm. Montcalm believed that the best way to defend the vital portage link between Lake George and Lake Champlain was to make a stand on the Heights of Carillon, a position about a half-mile from the fort. He ordered his men to the heights, where they felled trees and built a log wall nearly one mile long and between eight and nine feet high, backed by a *banquette* to raise men up to firing height. The French soldiers topped the

NEW RESIDENTS
A young red fox scouts the stone foundations of His Majesty's Fort at Crown Point, right. The foxes have taken to denning in the ruined forts at Crown Point State Historic Site and are often seen wandering among the rubble.

four-square-mile historic site preserved at Fort Ticonderoga. Remnants of Montcalm's wall, considered the best-preserved French earthworks in North America, are still visible today. By the tree-lined driveway that leads up to the fort stands a wooden cross, a reconstruction of the one erected by Montcalm after the rout.

COUP DE GRÂCE

Despite Montcalm's victory it had become clear that nothing short of a miracle would stop New France from crumbling. In July 1759 a British army of about 11,000 men marched on Carillon. The outnumbered French garrison withdrew up the lake. Three French deserters told the British that the French soldiers had left behind a fuse set to blow up the fort. Major General Jeffrey Amherst, who had replaced Abercrombie, tried to persuade one of the deserters to lead the British to the fuse, offering a reward of 100 guineas, but no one accepted. Two hours later an explosion

rent the air, followed by a raging fire that burned unchecked for several days. When British soldiers were finally able to investigate the ruins, they found that the powder magazine, the east curtain wall, and the woodwork of the soldiers' barracks had all been destroyed. But the garden had survived the blast. One soldier noted that the cabbage "is very plenty and all sorts of greens which they got in the French garden. They had a fine garden large anuf to give the whole army a mess."

The war over the lake corridor had ended. The British followed the retreating French army to Fort St. Frédéric only to find that they had blown it up as well. Amherst dug in and ordered his men to erect His Majesty's Fort of Crown Point near the French fort's ruins. The following summer troops from Crown Point participated in a concerted attack on Montreal that toppled New France. The Treaty of Paris was signed three years later, thus setting the American colonies on the path toward independence from Britain.

MILITARY MIGHT
The soldiers' quarters at His Majesty's Fort of Crown Point, above, is one of three barracks that were designed to accommodate 4,000 men. The massive fort was part of a three-and-a-half-square-mile fortification complex that included three redoubts and a series of blockhouses connected by roads. Surrounded by 6- to 15-foot-high stone foundations that were topped by another 27 feet of wooden crib-work filled with earth, the fort served as a standard of British military might from 1759 to 1775.

NEARBY SITES & ATTRACTIONS

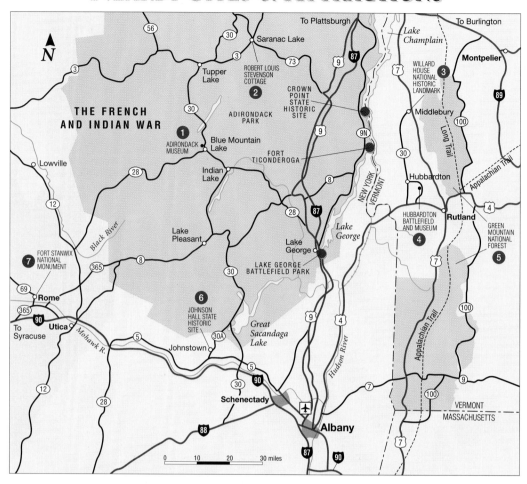

Legend has it that the first time the Stars and Stripes flew in battle was at Fort Stanwix, below, during a three-week siege in 1777.

1 ADIRONDACK MUSEUM, NEW YORK

As a playground to millionaires, health retreat for tuberculosis sufferers, and centuries-old hunting ground, the Adirondacks boast a rich history. Visitors to this unique museum can tour 22 indoor and outdoor exhibits, ranging from full-scale cottages to displays devoted to boating in the Adirondacks. Other highlights include the Wilderness Cure exhibit, which describes the tuberculosis sanatoriums in the region; a series of displays concentrating on camping, surveying, and hunting; an exhibit that focuses on the history of logging; and more than 160 vintage photographs of the area. Located one mile north of Blue Mountain Lake on Hwy. 30.

2 ROBERT LOUIS STEVENSON COTTAGE, NEW YORK

This cottage allows visitors a glimpse of the private man behind the writer who brought readers *The Strange Case of Dr. Jekyll and Mr. Hyde.* The cottage, which Stevenson occupied in the winter of 1887–88, has been preserved in the state in which he left it, right down to the cigarette burns on the wooden mantelpiece over the fireplace. Other mementos on display include the writer's smoking jacket, childhood photographs, a lock of his hair, and several original letters. Located on Stevenson Lane in Saranac Lake.

3 WILLARD HOUSE NATIONAL HISTORIC LANDMARK, VERMONT

Emma Hart Willard was a pioneer of women's education. She opened the Middlebury Female Seminary at her home in 1814 in order to augment her husband's income. Willard soon realized that her pupils could benefit from the higher education offered at nearby Middlebury College and asked the college president if her pupils could attend classes there. The request was denied, igniting Willard's battle for a woman's right to a college education. Willard wrote her *Plan for Improving Female Education* in this Federal-style house, which has been refurbished and is currently used as Middlebury College's admissions and financial aid office. The house was declared a National Historic Landmark in 1966. Located on the campus of Middlebury College.

4 HUBBARDTON BATTLEFIELD AND MUSEUM, VERMONT

This is the site of the only Revolutionary War battle fought entirely in the state of Vermont. On July 7, 1777, a combined force of British and German troops was advancing on American major general Arthur St. Clair and his men as they retreated from Fort Ticonderoga and Mount Independence after losing to the British. St. Clair left 1,200 of his men in Hubbardton, including the Green Mountain Boys, to defend the retreating forces from attack. In what is considered to be a great rear-guard action, the small American detachment, positioned on Monument Hill, delayed the enemy forces long enough to allow the main body of the American army to escape and regroup. A visitor center features dioramas and a fiber-optic map that displays the highlights of the battle. Located east of Hubbardton off Hwy. 4.

5 GREEN MOUNTAIN NATIONAL FOREST, VERMONT

Two National Scenic Trails, the Appalachian and the Long, meander through this 359,000-acre park. Hikers can climb to the summit of 4,052-foot Mount Abraham or take a short, steep hike up Mount Horrid, where hawks can be seen spiraling in

the sky overhead. A drive along Hwy. 100 affords motorists the opportunity to take in the terrain's many scenic splendors. Also located here is the Sugarbush Valley Ski Area, a popular downhill ski resort. The forest headquarters are in Rutland.

6 JOHNSON HALL STATE HISTORIC SITE, NEW YORK

This Georgian mansion, which dates from 1763, was owned by wealthy businessman Sir William Johnson, whose great rapport with the local Iroquois helped forge trading bonds that became vital in the French and Indian War. His Native American allies, including Indian leader Joseph Brant, assisted the British in defeating the French at the Battle of Lake George. Johnson, who was a staunch loyalist, died before the Revolutionary War broke out. At that time, his family, including Joseph Brant's sister, Molly, mother of nine of Johnson's children, was forced to flee to Canada. Their mansion was subsequently confiscated by the state of New York and put up for auction. The house remained a private residence until 1906, when it was named a historic site. Today visitors can tour the house and a collection of historical artifacts. Located on Hall Ave. in Johnstown.

7 FORT STANWIX NATIONAL MONUMENT, NEW YORK

The fort was abandoned by its British owners in 1763 and then rebuilt by patriot soldiers after the Revolutionary War began. During a three-week siege in 1777, a force of 550 Americans successfully defended the fort against 1,700 British and Indian troops. Leveled by the 1830's, the fort was reconstructed in the 1970's. Visitors can tour the site and see a portion of the more than 100,000 artifacts that have been recovered here. Located in Rome.

Spectacular scenery, such as beautiful Grout Pond with its muted colors, above, draws visitors to Green Mountain National Forest.

Johnson Hall, left, the home of Sir William Johnson, welcomed Native Americans and travelers from around the world. There was no household schedule; guests were instructed to entertain themselves in whatever manner they pleased.

WAR IN PENNSYLVANIA

The Continental Army was toughened by battle and terrible hardship in the Pennsylvania countryside.

For the first 18 months or so of the American Revolution, Pennsylvania escaped relatively unscathed from the frenzied violence that tore away at Massachusetts, North Carolina, and New York. On the western bank of the Delaware River life went on as usual despite the ominous rumblings of the bitter war. Colonists like Robert and Hannah Thompson went about their daily chores in their spacious stone farmhouse. Farther west, near Brandywine River, pacifist Quakers attended services at the Birmingham Meeting House; and just south of the Schuylkill River, a businessman named Isaac Potts worked his iron forge.

The peace reigning over this idyllic scene was not destined to last. Like a swiftly moving fog, the horrors and depredations of the cataclysmic conflict would engulf the Pennsylvania countryside as the British moved in to take the Colonial capital of Philadelphia.

In the fall of 1776, unbeknownst to the inhabitants of the region, Gen. George Washington was leading his ragged Continental Army in a hasty

HISTORIC HEADQUARTERS
Overleaf: A blanket of snow covers George Washington's Headquarters at Valley Forge National Historical Park. Originally the home of local blacksmith and businessman Isaac Potts, the comfortable stone house was occupied by George and Martha Washington during the winter of 1777–78.

retreat across the New Jersey colony to the safety of the Delaware riverbank. The mighty British forces, nipping at Washington's heels, pursued them with confidence, having just routed the Americans in battles on Long Island and in Manhattan. As his troops swooped in for the coup de grâce, British commander Sir William Howe sensed that victory was close at hand.

CROSSING THE RIVER

On the night of December 8, 1776, Washington ordered his troops to cross the Delaware River, making sure that no boats were left on the New Jersey shore that could be used by the British to follow them.

By putting the Delaware between his men and Howe, however, Washington did little to relieve his growing anxiety. His tattered ranks had been reduced by 2,000 men when the troops' enlistment ran out at the end of November and they went home. And by New Year's Eve, another large batch of soldiers would complete their tour of duty.

"I have no doubt but General Howe will still make an attempt upon Philadelphia this Winter," the general wrote to his brother from his headquarters near present-day Washington Crossing, Pennsylvania. "I foresee nothing to oppose him a fortnight hence, as the time of all the Troops, except those of Virginia now reduced almost to nothing, and Smallwood's Regiment of Maryland, equally as low, will expire before the end of that time. . . . I think the game is pretty nearly up."

Washington deployed his regiments along the water's edge for some 20 miles from Dunk's Ferry in the south to Coryell's Ferry in the north, ready to meet the anticipated assault. He detailed Gen.

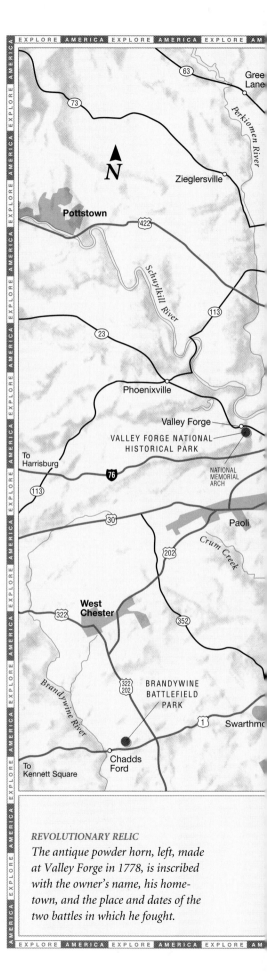

REVOLUTIONARY RELIC
The antique powder horn, left, made at Valley Forge in 1778, is inscribed with the owner's name, his home-town, and the place and dates of the two battles in which he fought.

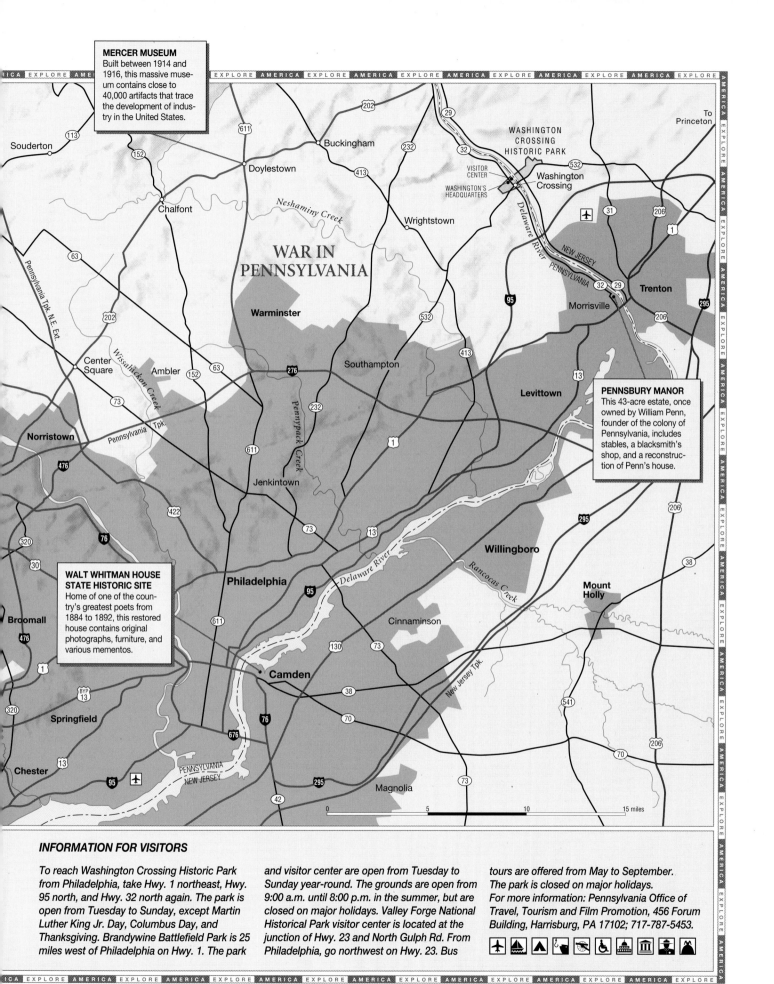

MERCER MUSEUM
Built between 1914 and 1916, this massive museum contains close to 40,000 artifacts that trace the development of industry in the United States.

WAR IN PENNSYLVANIA

PENNSBURY MANOR
This 43-acre estate, once owned by William Penn, founder of the colony of Pennsylvania, includes stables, a blacksmith's shop, and a reconstruction of Penn's house.

WALT WHITMAN HOUSE STATE HISTORIC SITE
Home of one of the country's greatest poets from 1884 to 1892, this restored house contains original photographs, furniture, and various mementos.

INFORMATION FOR VISITORS

To reach Washington Crossing Historic Park from Philadelphia, take Hwy. 1 northeast, Hwy. 95 north, and Hwy. 32 north again. The park is open from Tuesday to Sunday, except Martin Luther King Jr. Day, Columbus Day, and Thanksgiving. Brandywine Battlefield Park is 25 miles west of Philadelphia on Hwy. 1. The park and visitor center are open from Tuesday to Sunday year-round. The grounds are open from 9:00 a.m. until 8:00 p.m. in the summer, but are closed on major holidays. Valley Forge National Historical Park visitor center is located at the junction of Hwy. 23 and North Gulph Rd. From Philadelphia, go northwest on Hwy. 23. Bus tours are offered from May to September. The park is closed on major holidays.
For more information: Pennsylvania Office of Travel, Tourism and Film Promotion, 456 Forum Building, Harrisburg, PA 17102; 717-787-5453.

From astride his white mount, a somber George Washington looks over his beleaguered army in W. T. Trego's painting The March to Valley Forge, *right.*

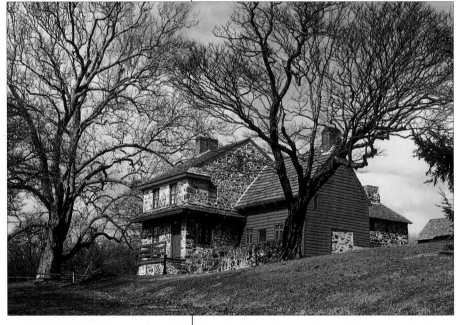

In 1777 the 19-year-old Marquis de Lafayette sailed from France to America to fight alongside the colonials. The aristocrat stayed in the fieldstone home of Gideon and Sarah Gilpin, above, near the site of the Battle of Brandywine.

William Alexander, commander of a division of Virginia, Delaware, and Maryland regiments, to guard a stretch of the river near McConkey's Ferry. A resident of New Jersey before the war, Alexander knew the area well and posted lookouts atop Bowman's Hill, the highest ground on the western side of the river. In winter this heavily wooded summit affords a good look at the surrounding country. Visitors can take an elevator to the top of a sturdy 110-foot-tall tower built in 1930 for an even more expansive vista.

KEEPING WATCH

During the siege, the sentries that kept watch from the summit had little trouble seeing through the bare branches to New Jersey on the other side of river. The general set up his headquarters less than a mile upstream at farmer Robert Thompson's house, which can be toured today along with several restored farm outbuildings in the Thompson's Mill section of Washington Crossing Historic Park.

For two dreary weeks, Washington's army vigilantly scanned the opposite riverbank, but the attack never materialized. After a perfunctory search for boats along the New Jersey shore, General Howe ordered his army into winter quarters. Washington counted the days until his troops' tour of duty would expire. On December 22 he lamented: "By the first of next month then, we shall be . . . reduced so much by sickness . . . as in the whole not to exceed, but short of 1,200 men. Upon these and the Militia, is all our dependence, for you may as well attempt to stop the Winds from blowing, or the Sun in its diurnal, as the Regiments from going when their term is expired."

In council with his officers, the general decided to cross back over the river and attack the British garrison at Trenton, New Jersey, trusting that "some lucky Chance may yet turn up" to grant him victory and boost the flagging morale of his men before they marched home. By some accounts, Washington fortified himself that Christmas night with an evening meal at McConkey's Ferry Inn,

BRAVERY REMEMBERED
A soft sunrise serves as a backdrop to the National Memorial Arch, below, dedicated in 1917. The monument is inscribed with Washington's words of praise for the "patience and fidelity" of the Revolutionary soldiers who braved the brutal conditions at Valley Forge in the winter of 1777–78.

located less than 100 yards from the site of the crossing. Hundreds of soldiers, their feet wrapped in rags, trudged through heavy snow to the water's edge. Today a bridge spans the river, but in 1776 the only way across was by boat.

The most serviceable vessels that Christmas were Durham boats, large flat-bottomed barges between 40 and 60 feet long, made for hauling heavy loads of iron ore along the river. Once a common sight on the Delaware, now only a handful of replicas are kept in a boathouse adjacent to the inn. The boats are used during the annual reenactment of the crossing every December.

Displacing less than two feet of water, the boats were extremely mobile. Amid blinding snow and shifting winds, boatmen from Marblehead in the Massachusetts regiment, rowed the army and all its artillery across to Trenton. Washington's bold move caught the German mercenaries guarding the garrison flat-footed. Surrounded by the colonials, the disorganized Hessian resistance withered beneath lethal musket fire. At battle's end nearly 1,000 Germans had been captured.

Less than a week later, Washington surprised and routed British reinforcements in Princeton when he deftly maneuvered his troops in the dark of night and won the short but fierce engagement. The British were driven out of most of New Jersey, prompting a rush of new colonial recruits.

The following spring, General Howe reformulated his plans to take Philadelphia. With the land route to Pennsylvania's front door barred by the

BATTLING WINTER'S CHILL
Costumed interpreters at Valley Forge National Historical Park, right, brace themselves against the cold. The staff and volunteers are far more warmly dressed than most of the unfortunate soldiers who spent the winter of 1777–78 here, many of whom didn't even own a pair of shoes.

COUNTRY CHARM
A rustic springhouse, below, located within Brandywine Battlefield Park dates to the 1740's. The stone structures, common to the region, were built above freshwater springs.

Delaware, he decided to thrust his army's full weight against the backdoor route from the sea. Howe boarded his regiments on naval vessels and sailed up Chesapeake Bay to Head of Elk, Maryland, approximately 50 miles southwest of Philadelphia. But Washington had anticipated Howe's gambit. He marched his troops westward and positioned them along the eastern bank of Brandywine Creek some 40 miles northeast of Head of Elk, behind a crossing known as Chadds Ford.

BLEAK OUTLOOK The prospects for defending their position did not look good to the Continental Army in September of 1777. The Brandywine River was a much less imposing barrier than the Delaware and could be forded in several places. Washington split his army to guard what he thought were all possible crossings. A two-story stone farmhouse behind the crossing was turned into his headquarters. (The existing headquarters was partially rebuilt following a ruinous fire.) A newly arrived French volunteer to the Revolutionary cause, the dashing Marquis de Lafayette, also found lodging nearby. Lafayette's quarters have survived virtually unchanged.

On the morning of September 11, 1777, the British set out from Kennett Square to Brandywine along present-day U.S. Route 1. Against all military strategic wisdom, Howe divided his army when it was in proximity to the enemy. But he deliberately

devised the risky plan of battle in the knowledge that his troops outmatched Washington's both in experience and number. He sent only about a third of his troops on a direct march toward Chadds Ford. Personally taking command of the remainder of his men, Howe marched north along Great Valley Road to a ford, unknown to Washington, that had been left undefended. From there, Howe swung his troops into position to attack the unsuspecting American forces from the rear.

The smaller British column advanced as conspicuously as possible, skirmishing along the way in an attempt to convince Washington that the entire British army was preparing to cross at Chadds Ford. The mission was a dangerous one: if Washington learned of the plan, he could counterattack and destroy the British detail before Howe had his men in position.

The American commander was given just this opportunity shortly after 10:00 a.m. Two scouts patrolling west of Brandywine spotted Howe's column. Washington seized the moment to overwhelm the British troops at Chadds Ford. He ordered Gen. Nathanael Greene's division, mostly Virginians, to cross the creek and attack.

The assault got off to a promising start, with Greene's forces driving enemy soldiers from the hills surrounding Chadds Ford. At this point, a third intelligence report reached Washington from an officer who had ridden the length of the Great Valley Road without so much as glimpsing the British column, which had been seen earlier. The scout's report was absolutely correct: Howe was no longer on the road; he had already forded the creek and was resting his troops on the other side before mounting his attack. However, when Washington heard this report, he lost his nerve. Fearful that he might have sent Greene off to fight the entire British army, Washington quickly ordered him back across the creek and into a reserve position behind Chadds Ford.

A little after midday, American patrols spotted Howe's column once again and rushed to tell Washington. The Continental Army thwarted disaster by swinging around to face the British on and around the grounds of the Birmingham Meeting House. A pitched battle followed, in which each side alternately gained the upper hand, with the redcoats finally driving off the Americans. As night fell, Washington's army retreated down the road to Chester. The British army swept through Paoli and marched into Philadelphia.

Today the land on which this pivotal battle was fought is privately owned. It is commemorated at the Brandywine Battlefield Park, located between Lafayette's quarters and Washington's headquarters on 50 acres of land east of the creek. Changing

exhibits at the park's visitor center relate the events that led up to the battle and describe the ebb and flow of the fighting itself and its aftermath.

PIVOTAL FIGURES
The statue of Baron von Steuben, above, gazes down at visitors to Valley Forge. Unlike many of his peers, von Steuben did not distance himself from the common soldier. He drilled them himself and chastised fellow officers who treated their men with disrespect. The baron and Washington often conferred at the commander in chief's reconstructed headquarters at Valley Forge, left.

WINTER HARDSHIPS

After Philadelphia was taken on September 26, Washington had to decide where his troops would camp over the winter. Some of his officers recommended Wilmington, Delaware, or Reading, Pennsylvania. Both sites did offer comfortable housing and relative safety from British attack. But other officers, and members of

SOLDIERS' MODEST QUARTERS
Visitors to Valley Forge can peer into replicas of the soldiers' huts, above, with their cramped living quarters. The men attempted to weatherproof the log cabins against the harsh winds and bitter cold by filling gaps in the walls with clay.

Congress, felt that stationing the army so far from Philadelphia would amount to ceding prosperous farmland to the British without a fight. Colonial authorities in Pennsylvania warned Washington that if he failed to protect the eastern part of the state, they would recall the Pennsylvania regiments—almost a quarter of the army.

The crux of the problem was that no suitable quarters existed close to Philadelphia. In addition, if the army encamped near the city it would be within an easy march of the enemy and, therefore, under a constant threat of attack. So Washington chose a site on the south bank of the Schuylkill River some 30 miles from Philadelphia. Known as Valley Forge, after Isaac Potts' iron forge, the area was not a valley at all, but a series of ridges and hills that served as a superb defensive strongpoint. Some historians believe it was military engineer Louis Duportail who first recommended Valley Forge to Washington. Others point to Anthony Wayne, a Pennsylvania general who is depicted in an impressive equestrian statue that overlooks the part of Valley Forge National Historical Park occupied by his 1st Pennsylvania Brigade.

On December 19, Washington marched his exhausted army into Valley Forge. He established his headquarters in Potts' stone house, where visitors can view furnishings typical of the era. A visitor center displays a collection of 18th-century weapons and accoutrements, and Washington's sleeping marquee.

Soldiers at Valley Forge didn't enjoy any comforts when it came to their housing. In a race against the impending bite of winter, squads of men cut down trees and hastily erected crude huts. A line of entrenchments guarded the encampment from attack, but the living quarters provided little protection against frigid winds and frost. Most of the huts fell apart after a year or two.

The primitive huts that stand in the park today are more sturdily built than the original structures they are meant to replicate, to ensure that they will survive as semipermanent features of the park. The 30 or so reconstructed huts represent a fraction of the 1,200 or more that were built during the winter of 1777–78. The timber needed for the huts denuded Mount Joy of its trees, and whatever wood was not used for the huts quickly went up in smoke as the men tried vainly to ward off the cold. Inside these shelters, poorly equipped soldiers huddled together for warmth, many of them lacking even basic items of clothing. With no money for real uniforms or shoes forthcoming, the men stood guard in the fierce wind wrapped in rags and blankets pooled from the dozen soldiers quartered inside each hut. About 2,000 troops died of exposure or illnesses such as dysentery and pneumonia during the encampment. The general's admiration for their courage is reflected in his words, inscribed on the National Memorial Arch: "Naked and starving as they are, we cannot enough admire the incomparable patience and fidelity of the soldiery."

PRECISION DRILLS

Much of the Grand Parade grounds remains a vast clearing. Here the army's newly appointed inspector general, Friedrich von Steuben, turned a shivering group of poorly trained soldiers into a formidable military beast. Many of the recruits did not know how to perform basic military maneuvers, such as marching in columns. Von Steuben drilled the troops twice a day, instructing his charges in European military techniques. Perhaps even more than Washington, von Steuben was the hero of Valley Forge, and a monument to the Prussian officer has pride of place, overlooking the parade grounds from an adjacent hill.

By hemming in the British forces in Philadelphia, the Continental Army denied them access to the countryside and made it hard for them to obtain supplies. By June 1778, British troops began evacuating Philadelphia to march toward New York, where their position was more firmly entrenched. On June 19, Washington and his men, once an army on the run, broke camp and gave chase. The tide had turned, and the hunted now tracked the hunter. Five years later the Continental forces would at last defeat the British.

No decisive battles were ever fought at Valley Forge, and no brilliant military schemes were hatched here to drive the redcoats from American soil. But the winter proved to be a catalyst, turning a weary band of ragtag Colonial soldiers into a determined and disciplined fighting force. Many soldiers died horrible deaths in that unforgiving season, but those who survived emerged stronger and more dedicated to the Revolutionary cause. Valley Forge National Historical Park and the battlegrounds of Pennsylvania stand as a testament to the lessons taught by hardship—lessons that helped forge a brave new nation.

HISTORIC ROW REENACTED
Interpreters dressed in period clothing restage Washington's dramatic crossing of the Delaware River every December, below. In 1776 Colonial forces contended with massive sheets of ice in the river as they launched their surprise attack on the British garrison at Trenton.

WINTER OF DISCONTENT
A replica of a soldier's hut at Valley Forge, left, is buffeted by howling winter winds such as those that decimated the ranks of the Continental Army in 1778. Each single-room log hut was 14 feet wide, 16 feet long, and just over 6 feet high.

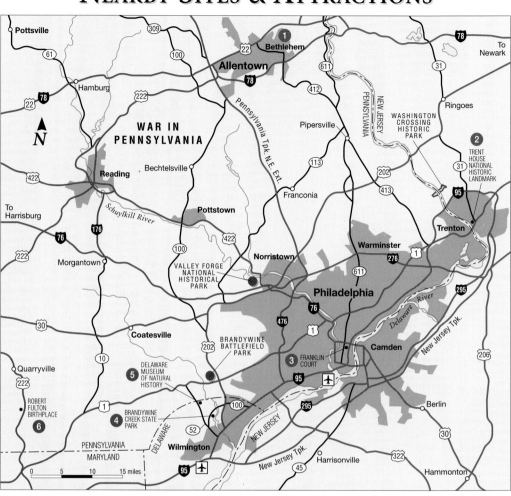

Tours of the Colonial-style kitchen and living room at the Robert Fulton Birthplace, above, are offered every weekend, Memorial Day through Labor Day, by volunteers from the local historical society.

1 BETHLEHEM, PENNSYLVANIA

A five-point star, visible from 20 miles away, adorns South Mountain and beckons visitors to Bethlehem, known as Christmas City U.S.A. The town, which is steeped in religious and musical tradition, was founded in 1741 by Moravians from Bohemia and Saxony in present-day Germany. Legend has it that a Moravian count, Nikolaus Ludwig von Zinzendorf, christened Bethlehem on Christmas Eve 1741, and ever since then the town has celebrated the holiday with annual Christmas pageants, feasts, and other celebrations. The Bach Choir of Bethlehem hosts a Bach festival each spring, based on a tradition of service in song that goes back to 1742. Several of Johann Sebastian Bach's most important works made their North American premieres in Bethlehem. The town's historic district features 21 buildings that predate the Revolutionary War. The five-story Gemeinhaus, the oldest structure in the town, was built of logs in 1741 and originally housed the entire community of Moravians. It now serves as the Moravian Museum on West Church St., and contains a collection of Moravian needlework, furniture, and silver. The stones marking the graves in the Moravian Cemetery are laid flat because of the Moravian belief that everyone is equal in life and in death. Located next to Allentown on Hwys. 22 and I-78.

2 TRENT HOUSE NATIONAL HISTORIC LANDMARK, NEW JERSEY

This mansion was built in 1719 by New Jersey's first chief justice, William Trent, who was also a successful businessman. When Trent moved to his estate, he dubbed the area Trent's Town. The restored Georgian-style house is furnished according to a 1726 inventory and features many unique pre-Revolutionary artifacts such as an Elizabethan game box, which contained several games. The cups in the Chinese tea set have no handles; instead tea was poured from the cup into the saucer and drunk from there. A chandelier has lift-off arms, which allowed household members to light their way in dark passages. Contrary to local custom, the kitchen, modern by pre-Revolutionary standards, was built indoors; kitchens were usually installed in another building to prevent fires spreading from the ever-burning hearth. Located at 15 Market St. in Trenton.

3 FRANKLIN COURT, PENNSYLVANIA

A modern structure of steel beams marks the site of Benjamin Franklin's last home, which was a 34-square-foot, three-story brick house. Lacking sufficient historical information to reconstruct the house, the National Park Service opted to build a frame on

The elegant Trent House dining room, left, reflects the tastes of pre-Revolutionary America. William Trent was able to afford a bathtub at a time when many people still bathed in rivers.

top of the old foundation, some of which is visible through the steel viewing tubes. An underground museum contains exhibits about Franklin and his family. After completing the house in 1765, Franklin spent 19 of the next 20 years away on diplomatic missions. When he finally returned to Philadelphia to live in 1785, he was 80 years old. Over the next five years, until his death, he added a library, two bedrooms, and two garrets to the house. The complex also comprises the Market Street Houses, which Franklin built and rented out. Today these buildings contain an 18th-century printing office, exhibits on architecture and archeology, a post office, and a postal museum. Located on Market St. between Third and Fourth Sts. in Philadelphia.

④ BRANDYWINE CREEK STATE PARK, DELAWARE

Native Americans settled in the region 12,000 years ago, drawn by the plentiful shad and herring in the area's many rivers. In the late 1600's Colonial settlers built dams, which disrupted the fish runs, and the Indians slowly ceased to hunt here. The region's first colonists built wood houses, but later settlers constructed their dwellings of stone. Some of the original stone farmsteads still stand and are in use today. In the 1880's Col. Henry A. du Pont expanded his estate to include most of what is now the park and used the land as a cattle farm until 1965, when it was sold to the state of Delaware. The park, which is open year-round, has 12 miles of hiking trails, and in winter visitors can sled or cross-country ski. It is also home to diverse wildlife, including deer, several bird species, and the elusive Muhlenberg bog turtle. The gray stone walls that stand in various places in the 1,000-acre park were built in the late 1800's by Italian masons hired by du Pont. Located three miles north of Wilmington on Hwy. 100.

⑤ DELAWARE MUSEUM OF NATURAL HISTORY, DELAWARE

Travelers looking for a hands-on natural history lesson will enjoy the museum's dioramas of mammals, birds, and seashells. In the Discovery Room visitors can examine and handle fossils, skeletons, and skulls and view a snakeskin, spiders, and sharks' teeth through the museum's microscopes. The permanent collection of numerous outstanding objects includes the world's largest bird's egg and a 500-pound clamshell. A simulated African watering hole, a barrier reef, and a host of common and extinct bird species provide glimpses of natural life from around the world. Along with its permanent exhibits, the museum offers weekly workshops on its rotating natural history displays. Located five miles northwest of Wilmington on Hwy. 52.

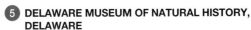

⑥ ROBERT FULTON BIRTHPLACE, PENNSYLVANIA

This restored fieldstone house is the birthplace of steamship pioneer Robert Fulton. Although he is remembered for his accomplishments as an engineer and an inventor, Fulton earned his living as an artist and has left behind numerous miniatures and portraits of prominent Philadelphians, including Benjamin Franklin. He was born in 1765 and launched his first steamboat, which he christened the *Clermont,* in 1807. He died in 1815 at the age of 49 before he could witness the launch of a steam-powered warship—the first of its kind—which he had designed for use in the War of 1812. Fulton's life and accomplishments are chronicled in one of the rooms in the three-story house. The 66 acres of surrounding farmland are leased to local farmers, who maintain the fields on the property. Located five miles south of Quarryville on Hwy. 222.

The steel structure, below, shows the dimensions of Benjamin Franklin's Philadelphia house, the only house he ever owned.

SURRENDER AT YORKTOWN

A Franco-American army defeated the British in the last battle of the War for Independence.

One of the best-preserved battlefields of the American Revolution survives in a tiny seacoast town in Virginia, site of a Civil War siege as well. The Colonial National Historical Park at Yorktown focuses on the decisive moment in the autumn of 1781 when allied American and French forces clashed with British soldiers in a battle that precipitated the end of the American War for Independence. On the outskirts of town, where meadows roll up to a 30-foot bluff above the York River and reconstructed American and French earthworks zigzag like raised green scars across the terrain, weary soldiers fought under a hailstorm of cannon and musket fire.

Today visitors bicycle or drive a seven-mile self-guided tour around the battlefield, pausing to read markers that indicate the positions of the American, French, and British soldiers. A visit to the park often concludes with a nine-mile tour of some of the important features of the Franco-

American encampment, such as the artillery parks where soldiers maintained and repaired the cannons, the grassy clearing among the hardwood trees where General Washington's tents were pitched, and the white cross that marks the burial place of some French soldiers killed in the siege.

The streets of Yorktown still follow their original 1691 mapping. Upscale shops, historic houses, and restaurants cluster around the town's working waterfront. Eighty percent of Yorktown's dwellings were damaged or destroyed during the allied siege. Of those that survived the war, only eight remain. One of them is the home of Thomas Nelson Jr., a signer of the Declaration of Independence and an ardent patriot who supported the American cause out of his own pocket. Nelson also served both as governor of Virginia and commander of its militia. Today costumed interpreters at the Thomas Nelson House reenact the days of the American Revolution as they argue the patriot and Tory positions. "True, the rag-tag and bob-tail troops are not as glorious as the Crown's," the actor who portrays Nelson passionately expounds. "But one Virginia long rifleman will outshoot a company of lobsterbacks on a Virginia field any day. Men fighting for their family, land and home become formidable foes." Fighting words indeed.

WAR WEARY BUT BATTLE-WORTHY

The American soldiers stationed along the Hudson River in 1781 did look ragtag and bobtail. They were frequently hungry, often ragged and barefoot as well; but even the splendidly outfitted French found them battleworthy—an extraordinary circumstance after six exhausting years of warfare.

The question as to which side would win the war was being reframed to ask which army would outlast the other. The effort of keeping the American army together through the long cold winter had been a significant accomplishment. By the spring of 1781, General Washington couldn't even afford to pay his troops, and most of the soldiers hadn't seen a payday in months.

When Washington wasn't worried about his beleaguered troops he was plotting out his summer campaign. He wanted to take New York City from the British, who had occupied it under Gen. Henry Clinton. But Washington's French allies, who were pumping critically needed troops, weapons, artillery, and ships into the Revolutionary cause, favored an offensive in Virginia.

On August 14, 1781, news reached Washington that the naval muscle he had been praying the French would provide—28 warships and 3,000 soldiers—was bound for the American coast. However, it was headed for Virginia's Chesapeake Bay, not New York, causing Washington to change his plans and turn his sights on Virginia.

To get his troops to the Chesapeake without drawing enemy fire, Washington proceeded to pull the wool over British eyes. According to one story, he spoke to an elderly New Yorker known to be a British spy and asked him several misleading questions, knowing his words would be repeated for enemy ears. He also issued orders for a decoy camp

FRIENDS FOR LIFE
The 95-foot Monument to Victory and Alliance in Yorktown, right, authorized by the Continental Congress on October 29, 1781, honors the partnership between the Americans and the French during the Revolutionary War. Work on the monument began in 1881, during the centennial of the victory at Yorktown, and was completed in 1884.

BRITISH CAPITULATION
Overleaf: The tidewater meadow where the British surrendered after the siege of Yorktown is now called Surrender Field. In the pavilion overlooking the field, visitors relive the moment of victory by listening to a stirring account of how the defeated British army marched along the road, now marked by split-rail fences, between the twin lines of American and French soldiers, and laid down their muskets in the meadow.

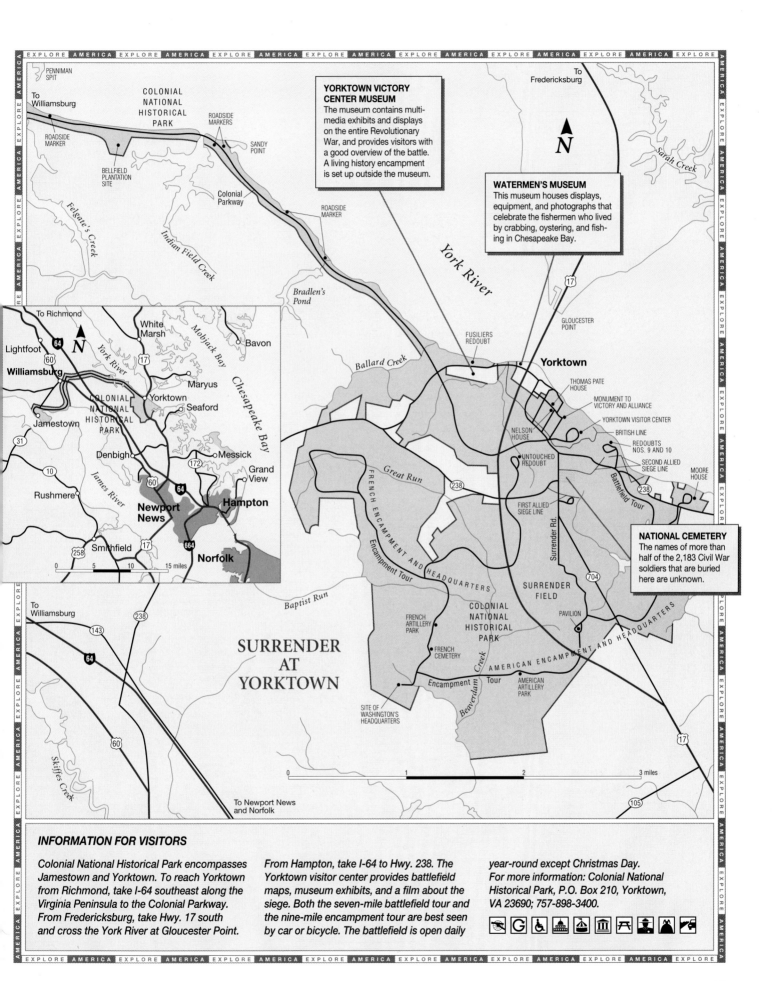

YORKTOWN VICTORY CENTER MUSEUM
The museum contains multimedia exhibits and displays on the entire Revolutionary War, and provides visitors with a good overview of the battle. A living history encampment is set up outside the museum.

WATERMEN'S MUSEUM
This museum houses displays, equipment, and photographs that celebrate the fishermen who lived by crabbing, oystering, and fishing in Chesapeake Bay.

NATIONAL CEMETERY
The names of more than half of the 2,183 Civil War soldiers that are buried here are unknown.

PENNIMAN SPIT

To Williamsburg

COLONIAL NATIONAL HISTORICAL PARK

ROADSIDE MARKERS

ROADSIDE MARKER

SANDY POINT

BELLFIELD PLANTATION SITE

Felgate's Creek

Indian Field Creek

Colonial Parkway

ROADSIDE MARKER

Bradlen's Pond

To Fredericksburg

N

Sarah Creek

York River

17

GLOUCESTER POINT

Ballard Creek

FUSILIERS REDOUBT

Yorktown

THOMAS PATE HOUSE

MONUMENT TO VICTORY AND ALLIANCE

YORKTOWN VISITOR CENTER

NELSON HOUSE

BRITISH LINE

REDOUBTS NOS. 9 AND 10

SECOND ALLIED SIEGE LINE

MOORE HOUSE

UNTOUCHED REDOUBT

Great Run

238

FIRST ALLIED SIEGE LINE

Battlefield Tour

238

To Richmond

White Marsh

Lightfoot

64

60

Williamsburg

York River

17

Mobjack Bay

Bavon

N

Maryus

COLONIAL NATIONAL HISTORICAL PARK

Yorktown

Seaford

Jamestown

31

Denbigh

James River

10

Rushmere

60

64

172

Messick

Grand View

Chesapeake Bay

Newport News

Hampton

258

Smithfield

17

664

Norfolk

0   5   10   15 miles

FRENCH ENCAMPMENT AND HEADQUARTERS

Encampment Tour

Baptist Run

To Williamsburg

238

143

64

60

Skiffes Creek

SURRENDER AT YORKTOWN

FRENCH ARTILLERY PARK

FRENCH CEMETERY

COLONIAL NATIONAL HISTORICAL PARK

Beaverdum Creek

Encampment Tour

SITE OF WASHINGTON'S HEADQUARTERS

Surrender Rd.

SURRENDER FIELD

PAVILION

704

AMERICAN ENCAMPMENT AND HEADQUARTERS

AMERICAN ARTILLERY PARK

17

105

To Newport News and Norfolk

0   1   2   3 miles

INFORMATION FOR VISITORS

Colonial National Historical Park encompasses Jamestown and Yorktown. To reach Yorktown from Richmond, take I-64 southeast along the Virginia Peninsula to the Colonial Parkway. From Fredericksburg, take Hwy. 17 south and cross the York River at Gloucester Point.

From Hampton, take I-64 to Hwy. 238. The Yorktown visitor center provides battlefield maps, museum exhibits, and a film about the siege. Both the seven-mile battlefield tour and the nine-mile encampment tour are best seen by car or bicycle. The battlefield is open daily

year-round except Christmas Day. For more information: Colonial National Historical Park, P.O. Box 210, Yorktown, VA 23690; 757-898-3400.

to be set up some 20 miles east of British head-quarters in New York City. Near this campsite of empty tents, a French crew built four huge brick ovens for baking army-size quantities of bread. Small detachments of soldiers were dispatched in directions that suggested they were preparing an attack on New York.

General Clinton took the bait and began forti-fying Manhattan. Nearly two weeks went by before he realized the allies had left the Hudson River val-ley and were on their way to Virginia.

Washington's troops—some 2,500 Americans, plus some 5,500 French soldiers under Count de Rochambeau—made up about half the entire allied army. Their destination was Yorktown, a tobacco port on Virginia's York River. In early August, Yorktown had been transformed into a naval and supply base by the British army under Lord Charles Cornwallis, commander of the southern forces. Cornwallis' force represented a third of the British army in North America; it numbered more than 8,300 men and included about 2,000 auxiliary troops from Germany, who were referred to as Hessians. The soldiers had subdued Georgia and parts of the Carolinas, and until recently, had been ravaging the Virginia countryside.

It took a month—from the middle of August until the middle of September—for the allied sol-diers to march from the Hudson Valley in New York to Virginia. On their way south they stopped in Philadelphia to plead with the Continental Congress for at least a small advance on their long-overdue pay. The bankrupt congress managed to raise enough cash to provide each American soldier with one month's salary—by borrowing the mon-ey from the French army.

As the armies marched, two French fleets con-verged on Yorktown. The larger of the two, with its 28 warships, was sailing north from the West Indies under the command of French admiral François de Grasse. The smaller one, sailing south from Rhode Island, was led by Adm. Saint-Laurent de Barras. His eight ships were loaded with 1,500 pounds of salt beef, as well as one vital type of car-go the British never expected to face at Yorktown—heavy siege cannons.

The allied generals learned to their horror that a third fleet was also headed toward Yorktown—that of British admiral Thomas Graves, whose 19 battleships had sailed out of New York Harbor. What if the British fleet reached the Chesapeake first? The thought was too terrible to entertain.

AERIAL VIEW
On October 14, 1781, French soldiers captured British redoubt No. 9, below. With the fall of this redoubt and the capture of redoubt No. 10 by the Americans, General Cornwallis became convinced that the battle of Yorktown was lost.

When the allied soldiers reached Chester, Pennsylvania, Count Jean de Rochambeau witnessed a remarkable sight: The normally reserved George Washington, clutching a hat in one hand and a handkerchief in the other, was swinging his arms in wide swooping circles. He grasped the French commander in a fierce embrace and shouted the news. De Grasse had made it into the Chesapeake first and his ships had set up a blockade! Cornwallis was now cut off from the sea.

On September 5, de Grasse sailed out to challenge Admiral Graves' fleet as it approached the Virginia coast. The outnumbered British fleet proved to be no match for the French navy and it was sent limping back to New York for repairs.

While the British and French fleets were battling it out, Washington received more welcome news: the eight ships of de Barras, carrying their precious cargo of beef and guns, had slipped through the Chesapeake and into the James River. Now it seemed to Washington that he couldn't get his troops to Yorktown fast enough. He knew he had to launch an attack before Clinton sent Cornwallis fresh supplies and reinforcements from New York. And he had only one month to complete the siege: de Grasse and his naval firepower were under orders to return to the Caribbean by mid-October.

At 5:00 a.m. on September 28, Washington commanded his troops to march the final 14 miles from Williamsburg to Yorktown. Washington's army was now swelled by the addition of some 3,500 Virginia militiamen, 2,500 Continental troops under the French general Marquis de Lafayette, and 3,000 French reinforcements under de Grasse. All together the American general now had 17,600 allied troops under his command.

Back in New York, Sir Henry Clinton seemed paralyzed by the news of his fleet's losses in the Chesapeake. On September 11, and again on the 24th, he sent more promises of ships and reinforcements to Cornwallis, but day after day, wracked with indecision, he failed to deploy them.

FORMIDABLE DEFENSES

Soon after the allied advance guard arrived at Yorktown, cannon and musket fire erupted from the British outer line. Peering through the trees, the allied soldiers could see the enemies' defenses: cannon batteries, V-shaped earthworks, called redans, and redoubts or earthen forts. Additional hazards had been added in the form of abatis, the 18th-century equivalent of barbed wire, made of tree branches woven tightly together, as well as fraises, sharpened tree trunks angled upward to impale onrushers.

Lord Cornwallis was optimistic about the outcome of the siege. The allied field artillery, he assured his officers, was too light to damage his fearsome defenses. The English navy would soon return to reassert its superiority.

While Washington and de Rochambeau conferred on how their soldiers would fight their way through the obstacle course of redoubts and redans, Cornwallis made an unanticipated decision. Banking on Clinton's promise to send reinforcements, he ordered a midnight retreat from his outer defense line and drew his men inward into a compact striking force behind his main inner line. Cornwallis felt that this line was easier to defend and that he needed to safeguard his men until

FATEFUL MEETING
A painting called The Stage Is Set, *above, which is on display at the visitor center at Yorktown, depicts the October 14 meeting between Washington and his staff to plan that evening's attack on British redoubts Nos. 9 and 10.*

AMERICAN CANNON
The reconstructed Grand American Battery contains several cannons mounted on carriages, such as the one shown at left.

The Thomas Pate House, right, located on Yorktown's Main Street, was built by a local ferryman named Pate. The house is being restored by the National Park Service.

Tours of Moore House, which are conducted by park rangers, include the Surrender Room, below, where the Articles of Capitulation for British Surrender were drafted on October 18, 1781. The house is situated about two miles outside Yorktown and was in Union hands in the spring of 1862 when it was damaged by Confederate artillery.

the reinforcements arrived. Visitors can still see the British inner defense line encircling the town.

The next morning the allies were at a complete loss to explain why the British had just handed them the outer defense line, as well as control of every road leading in and out of Yorktown. The retreat would give the American guns—once they were hauled into position—a clear field of fire into Yorktown. At noon the French and Americans moved into the now-vacated British positions and prepared to advance farther. French engineers mapped out siege lines, while enlisted men bundled sticks and crafted gabions, bottomless baskets to stabilize the soil used in the infrastructure of the earthworks. Once the earthworks were ready, they dragged up their heavy siege cannons.

Washington and de Rochambeau sent troops across the York River to Gloucester Point to hem in the British troops, who were dug in there, and to cut off supplies of fresh fodder for the enemy's horses. The result of their efforts became evident within days: rather than subject their horses to a slow death by starvation, the British killed them and threw their carcasses into the river.

Intermittent rainfall softened the ground, and on October 6 the Americans and French dug their first siege line, which was 2,000 yards long. The line went up in a single night, forming a wide crescent from Yorktown Creek to the banks of the York River. Four new redoubts, two protecting each flank, were thrown up along the line. Now the job of building gun emplacements proceeded at full speed. The soldiers dragged the mortars, howitzers, and siege guns into place and mounted them on carriages that could be tilted to lob their fire in a high arc into Yorktown.

On October 9 the first two allied batteries were completed and the honor of firing the first cannon was awarded to the French. Visitors can see the "first shot" battery on the western side of town. At about 5:00 that night, Washington struck the first match in an American battery, firing a shot that reportedly tore into the dining room of a house where British officers were eating dinner, upsetting plates and killing the commissary general.

Shots and shells whistled through the air all night, giving the British no time to repair their fortifications. The heavy barrage knocked out their cannons and shattered houses. By the following day, when Cornwallis received yet another dispatch from Clinton holding out a pledge of help, more than 60 massive allied guns were blasting metal into Yorktown and across the York River.

On October 11 the allies began digging a second parallel line that would bring them within 400 yards of the enemy's inner defenses and close enough for point-blank artillery fire. Two British advance

redoubts, Nos. 9 and 10, stood in the path of the digging. Four hundred American soldiers and about the same number of troops from the French army were elected to storm the redoubts with fixed bayonets. The European infantrymen, following traditional rules of warfare, stood their ground behind ax-wielding sappers, who hacked away at the fraises surrounding the targeted redoubt No. 9. The operation cost them time as well as lives—15 dead and 77 wounded—but eventually the soldiers reached the parapet and fired on their opponents, forcing them to surrender.

Redoubt No. 10, assigned to the Americans, was taken much more quickly. As the sappers marched forward to do their job, the light infantrymen, whooping and howling, stormed past them and charged through and around the fraises and up and over the parapets. Within minutes the British and Hessian soldiers dropped their weapons. The American dead came to 9, with 31 wounded.

Redoubts Nos. 9 and 10 were incorporated into the second siege line, now marked by park signs. Soldiers armed the line with heavy guns that wreaked havoc on the British defenses until not one of their cannons was left to return fire and only the mortars were operable.

Even the elements appeared to be enlisted in the fight for an American victory. When Clinton's long-awaited reinforcements finally stood ready to sail from New York Harbor, a giant black cloud suddenly materialized in the western sky and a violent storm blew in, damaging part of the fleet. Three days later, at midnight on October 16, Cornwallis loaded his troops onto flatboats, intending to secrete them across the York River and escape. Without warning, a freak storm rose up that, with-

in minutes, turned into a gale. The boats were driven back to shore by the churning water, right into the French naval blockade lying at the mouth of the York River.

The next morning Cornwallis conferred with his officers. The British had only 100 artillery rounds or so left. Smallpox had broken out in their camp and the hospital was crowded with the sick and wounded. The only humane thing to do was to request a cease-fire to discuss surrender terms.

SURRENDER WITHOUT HONOR

On October 18 the negotiators from both sides convened at the home of Augustine Moore to work out terms. The British were especially unhappy with one article under discussion: they would not be allowed to surrender "with the honors of war," a dignity the British had denied the defenders of Charleston, South Carolina, in May of that year. Hours of wrangling ensued but the Americans stood firm. Finally Cornwallis agreed and the combatants signed the document on the morning of October 19. Later that day, under a clear blue sky and the gaze of hundreds of civilians, the British army marched to a meadow about a mile and a half from their inner defense lines and laid down a mountain of rifles. The treaty acknowledging American independence wasn't signed until two years later, on September 3, 1783.

Visitors to Surrender Field can almost see the soldiers: the British in their crisp uniforms issued for the occasion; the French, resplendent in plumes and gold braid; and the Americans, their boots and guns polished but their uniforms worn to threads. Yet, the day—and the country—belonged to them.

Nearby Sites & Attractions

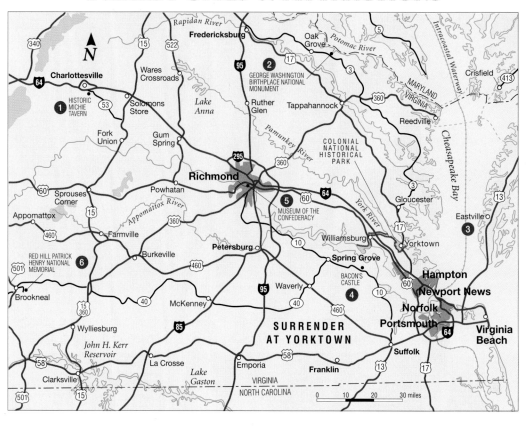

Next door to the Museum of the Confederacy in Richmond is the White House of the Confederacy, above, which served as the home of Confederate president Jefferson Davis during the Civil War.

❶ HISTORIC MICHIE TAVERN

Historic Michie Tavern, established in 1874 by Scotsman William Michie, offered food and lodging to travelers and served as the social center for the community. In 1927 the tavern, a prime example of the Colonial Revival style of architecture, was moved 17 miles to its present location about a half mile from Monticello. Today the tavern's dining room, called the Ordinary, features hearty lunch fare. Menu items date back to the 1700's and include Colonial fried chicken, black-eyed peas, and cornbread. Visitors can tour the original inn, dance the Virginia reel in the ballroom, and visit the gentlemen's parlor for a tankard of a delicious drink made from an 18th-century recipe. The tavern's outbuildings house the Virginia Wine Museum and the Grist Mill, both of which are open to the public. Located about a half mile south of Charlottesville off Hwy. 53.

❷ GEORGE WASHINGTON BIRTHPLACE NATIONAL MONUMENT

This 550-acre monument includes the birthplace of the nation's first president, an 18th-century plantation house, and a Colonial-era working farm. George Washington was born in 1732 in the home that his father, Augustine, built between 1722 and 1726. Washington lived there until the age of three, when he moved to Mount Vernon. The house was destroyed by fire on Christmas Day 1779, and only the foundations are visible today. Although no attempt has ever been made to build a replica of the original home, in 1931 a typical Colonial Virginia plantation home was

constructed on the site. The Colonial Living Farm, also part of the monument, features crops that were planted and harvested on Colonial farms. The Washington family cemetery is also located at the monument. Washington's father, grandfather, great-grandfather, and 27 other members of his family are buried here. Located 38 miles east of Fredericksburg off Hwy. 3.

❸ EASTVILLE

The town of Eastville has been the seat of government for Northampton County since 1715, and many of its residential and government structures date back to that time or earlier. Buildings of interest include the Colonial Courthouse, built in 1731, and the Northampton County Courthouse, whose records, dating back to 1632, are the oldest continuous court records in the nation. The Debtors Prison, built in 1644, is one of the nation's oldest such jails. It was enlarged in 1824, but became obsolete in 1873 when imprisonment for debt was outlawed. The structure served as a meeting place and a library until its conversion to a museum in 1953. In the prison yard is a whipping post dating to the 17th century. Located on Hwy. 13.

❹ BACON'S CASTLE

This restored two-story house was named after the fiery revolutionary Nathaniel Bacon, who led a revolt against British rule in 1676 and whose rebel force

Michie Tavern, left, maintained separate parlors for men and women so that ladies wouldn't be exposed to the evils of gambling and drink.

Bacon's Castle, below, is one of the oldest brick homes in the United States. It is owned and operated by the Association for the Preservation of Virginia Antiquities.

occupied the house for four months. It was built in 1665 by Arthur Allen, a Virginia colonist who became a prosperous merchant and planter. The house is unusually complex for a time when most homes were one-and-a-half-story timber frame structures. Built in the shape of a Greek cross, the national historic landmark features two sets of triple chimneys and curvilinear Jacobean gables. After touring the house, visitors explore the recently excavated 17th-century garden plot. Located off Hwy. 10 in Surry County.

5 MUSEUM OF THE CONFEDERACY

This museum's collection of Civil War battle flags, diaries, letters, photographs, rifles, pistols, cannons, and uniforms makes it one of the most impressive of its kind. Other items on display include Robert E. Lee's saddle, field glasses, bed, clothing, and the sword he wore when he surrendered to Ulysses S. Grant at Appomattox Court House. The sword, saddle, and plumed hat of cavalry commander J. E. B. Stuart, as well as the Bible carried by Thomas J. "Stonewall" Jackson, are also featured. Other exhibits document the lives of women and slaves of the era. Located at 1201 East Clay St. in Richmond.

6 RED HILL PATRICK HENRY NATIONAL MEMORIAL

This memorial is dedicated to Virginia's first governor, the famed lawyer and orator Patrick Henry, who is best remembered for his words "Give me liberty, or give me death." Henry lived in the modest frame house upon retiring in 1794 and he died five years later. The original structure burned to the ground in 1919, but a reconstructed house stands on the site, as well as the original carriage house, law office, kitchen, herb garden, and a boxwood maze. Also notable is a striking 64-foot-high Osage orange tree, and Henry's grave, which is marked with the simple words "His fame his best epitaph." Located five miles east of Brookneal off Hwy. 501.

BATTLE OF NEW ORLEANS

*America's greatest land victory
in the War of 1812 was the
last battle of the conflict.*

From downtown New Orleans, the road to the old plantation of Chalmette, where British and American soldiers clashed in the 1815 Battle of New Orleans, skirts the northern edge of the city's French Quarter and arcs through the old neighborhoods that crowd the shores of the Mississippi River. The road crosses a canal with a drawbridge and unrolls across a flat industrial area stitched together with railroad tracks and marked by the heavy metal of factories and oil storage tanks until it reaches the battlefield park. Once there, a National Park Service sign is the only outward indication that beyond the line of trees at the entrance lies the most storied killing field of the War of 1812.

At Chalmette the city seems oddly distant. The whiff of industry yields to the scent of wildflowers and the pervasive odor of the Mississippi River. The sound of traffic on the highway becomes a faint murmur behind the pinging beat of draw ropes that slap against two flagpoles. Like two sentinels, the poles face one another across a

acres of coastal wetlands south of the city; and Acadian cultural centers in Lafayette, Thibodaux, and Eunice, Louisiana. The visitor center for the Chalmette Battlefield Site is located between a war memorial, called the Chalmette Monument, and a shaded picnic ground that sprawls toward the river past the antebellum Malus-Beauregard House. Beside the entrance road, cannons peer over a long, earthen hump, their muzzles pointing toward the far end of the battlefield, where a low brick fence encloses Chalmette National Cemetery.

Visitors are often surprised by the small size of the battlefield. Somehow an immense theater seems a more likely setting for the dramatic fighting that ended in America's greatest land victory of the War of 1812—not this slender piece of land, 141 acres and perhaps 1,000 yards wide, wedged between a river levee and a cypress swamp. Yet it is precisely the narrow limits imposed by this geography that enabled Gen. Andrew Jackson and 5,500 regular militia and volunteer soldiers to repulse an experienced British army of 10,000.

ROOTS OF WAR

The attempt by the British to seize New Orleans by taking this narrow neck of land was characteristic of a war that began in confusion and divisiveness and was fought under conditions fraught with blunders and mayhem. Sometimes called America's second war for independence, the War of 1812 originated in the nation's attempt to remain neutral during England's long-running war with France. American merchant vessels were being harassed by both European powers, but because the British controlled the high seas, they posed a greater threat than did the French. At the same time, the British, leery of an expansionist United States that was covetous of their Canadian colony, informally encouraged and supported Indian hostilities against American settlers on the northwestern frontier.

The war was entered into halfheartedly by both sides on June 1, 1812. After years of failed diplomatic and economic efforts to coerce the British into halting its campaign of impressment and confiscation of American shipments, Pres. James Madison reluctantly called for a declaration of war. Although Congress granted the request by a narrow margin, it appropriated few funds to pay for a war. The regular army was to be reinforced at the whim of state militias, some of which were controlled by governors opposed to war. For their part, the British concentrated on the effort against France and devoted few resources to the American front.

At first the war was waged mostly with rhetoric and propaganda. But as hostilities mounted, several naval skirmishes broke out on the Great Lakes,

battleground that seems as fixed as a photograph. Their flags, the Union Jack and the Stars and Stripes, undulate in the breeze and help orient visitors who stroll among the moss-trimmed live oaks as they try to conjure up images of the terrible fighting that went on here.

The battleground within Chalmette makes up one section of the Jean Lafitte National Historical Park and Preserve, which also includes a visitor center in the French Quarter Site in downtown New Orleans; the Barataria Preserve Unit, 20,000

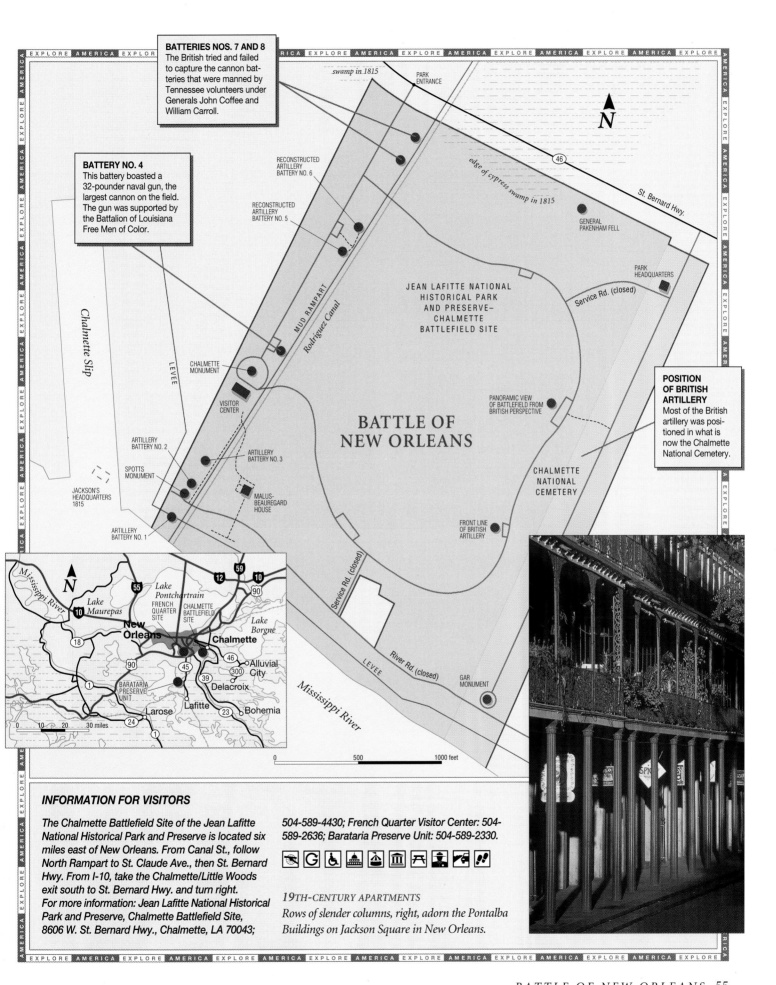

BATTERIES NOS. 7 AND 8
The British tried and failed to capture the cannon batteries that were manned by Tennessee volunteers under Generals John Coffee and William Carroll.

BATTERY NO. 4
This battery boasted a 32-pounder naval gun, the largest cannon on the field. The gun was supported by the Battalion of Louisiana Free Men of Color.

swamp in 1815

PARK ENTRANCE

N

46

edge of cypress swamp in 1815

St. Bernard Hwy.

RECONSTRUCTED ARTILLERY BATTERY NO. 6

RECONSTRUCTED ARTILLERY BATTERY NO. 5

GENERAL PAKENHAM FELL

PARK HEADQUARTERS

Chalmette Slip

MUD RAMPART

Rodriguez Canal

LEVEE

JEAN LAFITTE NATIONAL HISTORICAL PARK AND PRESERVE— CHALMETTE BATTLEFIELD SITE

Service Rd. (closed)

CHALMETTE MONUMENT

VISITOR CENTER

PANORAMIC VIEW OF BATTLEFIELD FROM BRITISH PERSPECTIVE

POSITION OF BRITISH ARTILLERY
Most of the British artillery was positioned in what is now the Chalmette National Cemetery.

BATTLE OF NEW ORLEANS

ARTILLERY BATTERY NO. 2

ARTILLERY BATTERY NO. 3

SPOTTS MONUMENT

CHALMETTE NATIONAL CEMETERY

JACKSON'S HEADQUARTERS 1815

MALUS-BEAUREGARD HOUSE

FRONT LINE OF BRITISH ARTILLERY

ARTILLERY BATTERY NO. 1

Service Rd. (closed)

N

Mississippi River

Lake Maurepas

55

Lake Pontchartrain

12

59

10

Lake Borgne

FRENCH QUARTER SITE

CHALMETTE BATTLEFIELD SITE

90

10

18

New Orleans

90

45

46

Chalmette

Alluvial City

300

1

BARATARIA PRESERVE UNIT

39

Delacroix

Larose

Lafitte

24

23

Bohemia

0   10   20   30 miles

Mississippi River

LEVEE

River Rd. (closed)

GAR MONUMENT

0   500   1000 feet

INFORMATION FOR VISITORS

The Chalmette Battlefield Site of the Jean Lafitte National Historical Park and Preserve is located six miles east of New Orleans. From Canal St., follow North Rampart to St. Claude Ave., then St. Bernard Hwy. From I-10, take the Chalmette/Little Woods exit south to St. Bernard Hwy. and turn right.
For more information: Jean Lafitte National Historical Park and Preserve, Chalmette Battlefield Site, 8606 W. St. Bernard Hwy., Chalmette, LA 70043;

504-589-4430; French Quarter Visitor Center: 504-589-2636; Barataria Preserve Unit: 504-589-2330.

19TH-CENTURY APARTMENTS
Rows of slender columns, right, adorn the Pontalba Buildings on Jackson Square in New Orleans.

and the British fended off several invasions of Canada, including one that led to the destruction of much of York (later called Toronto).

Then, in 1814, Napoleon abdicated. With the French defeated and an army of veteran British soldiers released from duty on the continent, the fighting picked up, and England turned its war machine on the United States in a three-point offensive. Some 15,000 British troops sailed to Canada, ending America's hope of conquest. Later in the year about 11,000 British troops crossed the border and invaded New York. But in August the Americans smashed the British naval force on Lake Champlain, forcing them back to Canada.

On August 24 another British force, fresh from a victory against American troops at the Battle of Bladensburg in Maryland, stormed Washington, D.C., setting fire to the Capitol, the White House, and other government buildings. In September, however, the British navy was turned back at Baltimore's Fort McHenry, and the army was stopped at North Point, also in Maryland.

The third offensive, which concluded with the Battle of New Orleans, began in December 1814 when a British fleet of more than 50 ships sailed into Lake Borgne, intent on taking New Orleans and closing the Mississippi to commerce.

The fleet deposited some 10,000 British soldiers on the shore. Under the command of Gen. John Keane, the army set out on foot for the short march

MONUMENTS TO THE PAST
The Malus-Beauregard House, above, dominates the battlefield's southwestern corner. The house, constructed in the antebellum style, was built 18 years after the battle. To the left of the house is the Chalmette Monument, which honors the American victory. Although its cornerstone was laid in 1840, the monument was not completed until 1908.

POISED FOR ACTION
In a print from the 1840's, right, Gen. Andrew Jackson is shown urging his men along Rodriguez Canal. The hodgepodge of American soldier uniforms in the depiction, though inaccurate, suggests the motley nature of the forces.

into the city. Who could stop them? They were experienced, highly disciplined soldiers commanded by professional officers with military skills honed in the long war with Napoleon.

General Andrew Jackson was in command of a far different army—a core of regular troops accompanied by militia, seamen, and citizen volunteers. He even had a few of Jean Lafitte's pirates straight out of prison. Jean Lafitte, the pirate for whom this national park and preserve is named, was operating from Barataria Bay when the British tried to recruit him—offering gold and a navy commission—for the attack on New Orleans. To their disappointment, Lafitte informed Jackson of the offer and then volunteered to help defend the city in exchange for the release from jail of his brother Pierre and some of his fellow buccaneers.

When Andrew Jackson learned that the British had landed on the shores of Lake Borgne, he was taken by surprise. He had expected the invasion to come by way of Mobile and was forced to scramble to adjust the positions of his troops.

The smart money would have been placed on the British. The troops encountered no resistance in the first few miles and probably could have reached the outskirts of the city with little effort. But the British advance force of 1,800 men halted nine miles from New Orleans and about three miles below Chalmette in order to await reinforcements and allow the men to rest.

Jackson, who rarely wasted an opportunity, took advantage of the delay by making a surprise move. As the British soldiers sat around their evening fires, he attacked the camp. Although the engagement was inconclusive, the British force was left shaken and their plans to advance effortlessly into New Orleans were thwarted.

The Americans fell back to Chalmette Plantation. The first line of defense, Jackson decided, would

be the Rodriguez Canal, a 1,200-yard-long man-made ditch that ran along the western boundary of the plantation from the river to the swamps. The ditch would hinder the British approach. Behind the ditch, Jackson had his men build a mud rampart, fortified with timber, across the entire breadth of the field. From there, infantrymen and cannoneers would have a nearly unobstructed view of anyone coming toward them.

RODRIGUEZ CANAL

Today Rodriguez Canal has mostly dried up and is overgrown with weeds. The cypress swamp that formed the northern boundary of the battlefield has long since been filled in, planted, or paved over. But a sense of the battle's scope can be gained from various vantage points along the one-and-a-quarter-mile road that loops through the battlefield.

Visitors standing near the remnants of the ramparts at Rodriguez Canal may try to imagine how it would have appeared, lined with soldiers and cannon, to troops tramping across the field of sugarcane stubble. Moving over to the British line, they can see just how difficult such an assault would be: a river levee lies to the left, swamps to the right, and 15 guns and thousands of muskets dead ahead.

In three engagements over a 12-day period, the British tried to make it through the canal's mud wall. The first attack took place on December 28, the day after Maj. Gen. Edward Pakenham replaced General Keane as the commander of the British forces. The battle began promisingly for the British, but ended in dismal failure. They deployed rockets, which they had used with devastating effect in earlier encounters with the Americans, and one column made good headway, but was then caught between the American line ahead and the armed schooner *Louisiana* on the Mississippi. The soldiers hurriedly took refuge in trenches that had been cut across the plain, standing in mud and icy water up to their waists. Pakenham ordered a general retirement that lasted for three days while he waited for his ships on Lake Borgne to deliver naval guns.

HERO OF SALAMANCA
Major General Edward M. Pakenham, left, took command of the British force on December 27, 1814. The brother-in-law of the duke of Wellington, he had earned a reputation for bravery for his part in the Battle of Salamanca, fought in Spain during the Peninsular War.

COASTAL WETLAND
Snakes, turtles, frogs, and alligators lurk in the cypress swamps of the Barataria Preserve Unit in the Jean Lafitte National Historical Park and Preserve, above.

On New Year's Day the Americans, peering through the fog, discerned three half-moon batteries positioned 600 yards away, each armed with heavy siege guns pointed right at them. All morning the opposing artillery waged battle, but by early afternoon it was clear that the British had been outshot and that the shoulder-high fortification along the canal had held firm.

On the foggy morning of January 8, Pakenham decided to go for broke. He threw 5,900 troops against the American line. The main thrust was aimed along the swamp to the left of the line. Another column attacked the high ground near the river levee. A third column remained in the rear near the Mississippi River, positioned to help either of the advance groups.

British soldiers charged along the river and briefly overpowered the rampart. But the main force near the swamps was being clobbered. In an attempt to aid them, General Keane formed a column of reinforcements of 978 Highlanders from the 93rd Regiment and marched them diagonally across the open cane field toward the swamp, directly in front of the American infantry and cannons. The troops were cut down by raking fire, and 578 of the Highlanders were killed or wounded. Keane

himself was hurt, but survived. Elsewhere on the battlefield, General Pakenham was struck twice after riding forward to organize his forces for a final, hopeless assault. The action failed, and the general died as he was carried off the field.

The Americans, who suffered only 71 casualties—13 dead, 39 wounded, and 19 missing or captured—were astounded by the number of bodies they found littered across the battlefield; the British counted 292 dead and 1,262 wounded in a battle that had lasted a mere two hours.

Thus the last war waged between Great Britain and the United States came to a close. The out-

come had far-reaching consequences. Although the treaty that officially ended the war declared it a draw, the American victory secured the nation's title to the Louisiana Territory in the eyes of the world, expedited the conquest of the West, and established the fledgling republic as an international power. Furthermore, the action at New Orleans gave the nation a new military hero, Andrew Jackson, who would go on to serve for two terms as the seventh president.

NEEDLESS FIGHTING

Unbeknownst to either side, the Battle of New Orleans was fought 15 days after representatives from both sides had met in Belgium and agreed to the terms of the Treaty of Ghent. Official notification of the treaty, which was ratified by Congress on February 18, 1815, reached Andrew Jackson on March 2. Had the Americans and the British known about the treaty, would they have clashed at Chalmette? Historians can only speculate about a different outcome. Later events have shown, however, that the War of 1812, and the final decisive engagement at New Orleans, pulled together a diverse citizenry and renewed the young republic's hard-won sense of nationhood.

REMINDERS OF WAR
During the Battle of New Orleans most of the British artillery was positioned in what is now the Chalmette National Cemetery, above. The cemetery is dedicated to veterans of all conflicts involving Americans. Of the 15,000 graves, only 4 date from the War of 1812 and just 1 veteran of the 1815 battle is buried here, a soldier who died on his way home to Tennessee.

NEARBY SITES & ATTRACTIONS

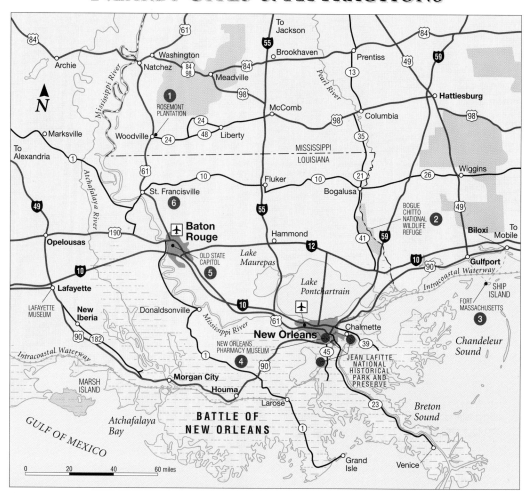

St. Francisville contains many fine examples of antebellum homes, such as the Rosedown Plantation, below. The house, which belonged to the Turnbull family for 120 years, contains all its original furnishings, as well as an impressive collection of historical documents. Outside, there is a 28-acre garden, first planted in the early 19th century.

① ROSEMONT PLANTATION, MISSISSIPPI

The home of Confederate president Jefferson Davis contains numerous family treasures and original furnishings. The Federal-style house was built in 1810 by Davis' parents, Samuel and Jane Davis, who harked from Kentucky, and was lived in by members of the Davis family until 1895. An antique four-poster bed that belonged to Jane Davis is on display in one of the bedrooms of the one-and-a-half-story planter's cottage. The family parlor is furnished with an 1805 side chair, an 1853 Pleyel piano, and a set of wooden candlesticks purported to have been carved by one of the servants and given to Jefferson Davis. The central hallway is lit by an 1843 chandelier that burns whale oil, and a display case in the hall contains a sword that Congress awarded Jefferson Davis for his valor in the Mexican War. Five generations of the Davis family are buried in the cemetery, including Davis' mother and two sisters. Located one mile east of Woodville off Hwy. 24.

② BOGUE CHITTO NATIONAL WILDLIFE REFUGE, LOUISIANA/MISSISSIPPI

This 36,000-acre refuge, encompassing rivers, oxbow lakes, swamps, and sandbars, is best viewed by canoeing along its more than 50 miles of waterways, portions of which have been designated as scenic rivers. Resident wildlife includes coyotes, wild turkeys, white-tailed deer, river otters, and beavers. The refuge is open to the public year-round. Located 60 miles northeast of New Orleans off Hwy. 41.

3 FORT MASSACHUSETTS, MISSISSIPPI

Situated at the western end of Ship Island at the entrance to the Mississippi Sound and Ship Island Harbor, Fort Massachusetts is an excellent example of a coastal defense of the Civil War period. The fort, built of brick, slate, and granite between 1859 and 1866, was controlled by the Confederate Army from the beginning of the Civil War to September 1861, when the Union Army took control and held it for the duration of the war. It was instrumental in the naval blockade against the Confederacy and in 1862, 20,000 Union troops were assembled on Ship Island prior to the invasion of New Orleans. Another 15,000 soldiers assembled here before the 1864 Battle of Mobile Bay. On display is a 15-inch Rodman gun, a powerful cannon with a barrel and carriage weighing more than 80,000 pounds. It fired 15-inch-diameter cannonballs weighing 440 pounds a distance of about three miles. Visitors can view the shot furnace where cannonballs could be heated before they were hurled at distant ships to set them on fire. A tour of the fort includes the rifle positions, guardrooms, casemates, and half bastions. The powder magazines, located next to the guardrooms, were lined with wood to help keep the gunpowder dry. Located on West Ship Island.

4 NEW ORLEANS PHARMACY MUSEUM, LOUISIANA

The museum is devoted to 19th-century medicine and pharmacology and is housed in an apothecary shop that dates to 1823. Named *La Pharmacie Française,* the shop was the first licensed pharmacy to open in the nation. The museum's 1850 cabinets hold herbs, potions concocted by voodoo practitioners, Civil War surgical equipment, leech jars, and bloodletting devices. Also on display are perfumes and face creams, once the specialty of pharmacists. Located on Chartres St. in New Orleans.

5 OLD STATE CAPITOL, LOUISIANA

This 19th-century structure, designed by the architect James Dakin, is considered one of the best examples of the Gothic Revival style in the United States. The original structure was built between 1847 and 1850, and after it was gutted by fire in 1862 it was rebuilt with red brick and stucco between 1880 and 1882. The front and rear facades are made of Missouri marble. The interior features brass chandeliers and pedestal lamps. Located in Baton Rouge.

6 ST. FRANCISVILLE, LOUISIANA

The second-oldest incorporated town in Louisiana has 146 historic buildings, some of which date from the 18th century. Highlights of St. Francisville's National Register Historic District include Our Lady of Mt. Carmel Catholic Church, which was built in 1871 from architectural plans by Confederate general P. G. T. Beauregard; and Propinquity, an 1809 house that is one of the city's oldest brick buildings. Located on Hwy. 61.

The Old State Capitol in Baton Rouge, above, displays castellated Gothic architectural features. The building was once known as the Castle on the Mississippi.

Excursion boats connect the mainland with Fort Massachusetts, left, on Mississippi's West Ship Island. Park rangers give guided tours of the fort during the summer.

FORT LARAMIE

*A crude trading post by the Laramie River on
Wyoming's northern Plains became one of the
key military forts on the Western frontier.*

Fort Laramie, best known as a military post, was established not by soldiers but by fur traders. Its rich history began with mountain men Robert Campbell and William Sublette, who hoped to make their fortune on the far-flung Western frontier by selling precious supplies at jacked-up prices to fellow trappers in the Rocky Mountains. By 1834 Sublette and Campbell were among the leading suppliers in the region. To further establish their hold on the fur trade, the pair built a trading post that served several routes to the West.

That spring Sublette headed for the annual trading rendezvous near the Idaho border, leaving behind 14 men to construct a fort along the far reaches of the North Platte River in what is now southeastern Wyoming. The log outpost, christened Fort William, after Sublette, was erected near a lazy loop on the Laramie River where it meets the North Platte. Its location was chosen deliberately to ensure Sublette and Campbell's continued dominance of the fur trade: it was the central location for the majority of the Plains Indian tribes for their trade in buffalo robes.

The bold venture paid off. More than 100 lodges of the Oglala branch of the Lakota, called the Sioux by their enemies, migrated to the North Platte near Fort William. For a year, Sublette and Campbell monopolized trade, amassing huge piles of buffalo robes that they exchanged for tobacco, sugar, liquor, blankets, and beads.

But competition in the fur trade was becoming increasingly fierce and in 1835 the enterprising team sold the fort to Fontenelle, Fitzpatrick and Company, who promptly renamed it Fort Lucien, after Fontenelle. The following year the powerful American Fur Company assumed ownership of the site. By 1840 the log structure had deteriorated badly and the American Fur Company was losing business to rival traders. In a decisive move to win back clients, the company replaced the log fort with an adobe complex and dubbed it Fort

BOOK LEARNING
*Fort Laramie's library stocked a few
hundred well-thumbed books such
as the ones on display at the site,
above. Titles included* Progressive
Intellectual Arithmetic *and*
Harvey's Elementary Grammar.

RESCUING THE PAST
*Overleaf: All but 1 of the 60 build-
ings at Fort Laramie were sold at
public auction in the spring of 1890;
some of the original structures were
stripped of their usable lumber
and left to deteriorate. The fort's
private dwellings, businesses, and
barns were in use until 1938, when
the restoration was initiated.
Authentic materials, including oak
dowels and square-cut nails, were
employed in the restoration, which
was completed in 1964.*

John. Traders and trappers called it "the fort on
the Laramie" or, more simply, Fort Laramie.

Over the next few years Fort Laramie became a
major fur-trade center. Furthermore, its strategic
position—at Mile 650 on the Oregon Trail, roughly midway between St. Louis and the Oregon border—meant that the fort became a principal layover
site for thousands of emigrants heading west.

Relations between the Lakota and the newcom-
ers were peaceful at first. But as a seemingly end-
less line of wagon trains gouged trails deeper into
the land, friction replaced tolerance. The great herds
of buffalo that had once roamed the Platte region
were driven away or killed off, their carcasses
allowed to rot on the plains, stripped of their hides,
their tongues cut out. In 1832, even before Fort
Laramie was built, itinerant artist George Catlin
was startled at the sight of more than 1,500 dead
buffaloes, slaughtered by Indians for the salted
tongues they would provide traders.

As the buffalo populations dwindled, life for the
Lakota situated near Fort Laramie became harder
and the Indians became more dependent on goods
supplied by the fort, including alcohol: liquor-
induced violence soon broke out among them. The
pioneers also imported silent killers: cholera, smallpox, and measles. One of the foremost tribes of the
Upper Missouri—the Mandan—was especially
hard hit by disease.

Parties of Lakota warriors, encamped along the
Oregon Trail, resorted to begging or bullying goods
from passing wagon trains. Complaints by emi-

grants and reports of rising tensions between them
and the Lakota prompted the federal government
to purchase Fort Laramie in 1849 and garrison it.
Barracks, stables, a bakery, and officers' quarters
were built around a central parade ground.

A SMALL GARRISON Fort Laramie National Historic
Site is a showcase restoration
representative of dozens of
long-gone Western military
posts. Today visitors to the fort, which is located
about 75 miles north of Cheyenne and 20 miles
northwest of Torrington, can amble across the central parade ground, wander along the banks of the
Laramie River where Campbell and Sublette erected their trading post, and peruse the collection of
artifacts in the site's museum.

Twelve of the structures in old Fort Laramie have
been restored. The interior of a rambling soldiers'
barrack is arranged as if ready for the troops to
return: weapons and uniforms await their owners,
bunks are made for inspection; the trappings of
military life lie about as if just put aside. More com-
fortably furnished are the officers' quarters, where
the homey signs of family life—a rocking chair and
a child's toy—serve as poignant reminders of the
wives and children who accompanied their hus-
bands to the Western frontier.

Beyond the nearby community of Fort Laramie
and past the farms and rangeland of Wyoming's
Platte and Goshen counties, the northern Plains
roll like a vast sea that reaches toward distant snow-
dusted peaks. Graceful pronghorn antelope bound
across the ridges, coyotes slink along the gullies,
hawks and eagles soar overhead, and this remarkable land's immense horizon seems to go on and
on. Fort Laramie and the surrounding landscape
would be recognizable today to the soldiers, settlers, and northern Plains Indians who knew it
during the tumultuous 19th century.

In the 1850's the army expected no trouble from
the Lakota, and Fort Laramie had only a small garrison and, like most major army posts in the West,
had no palisade to protect it from attacks. The
Indians soon realized that the troops had come to
the area not to protect them, but to serve the emi-
grant population instead. At first the Lakota were
too busy fighting their traditional enemies—the
Pawnee, Crow, and Shoshoni—to make war on
the pioneers traveling the Oregon Trail.

In a wrongheaded attempt to end the tribal warfare on the northern Plains and to extend federal
control over the warring tribes, Congress appropriated $100,000 in 1851 to convene a grand coun-
cil of the northern Plains tribes at Fort Laramie.
Messengers were dispatched to the tribes of the
Arkansas, Missouri, Yellowstone, and Platte rivers,

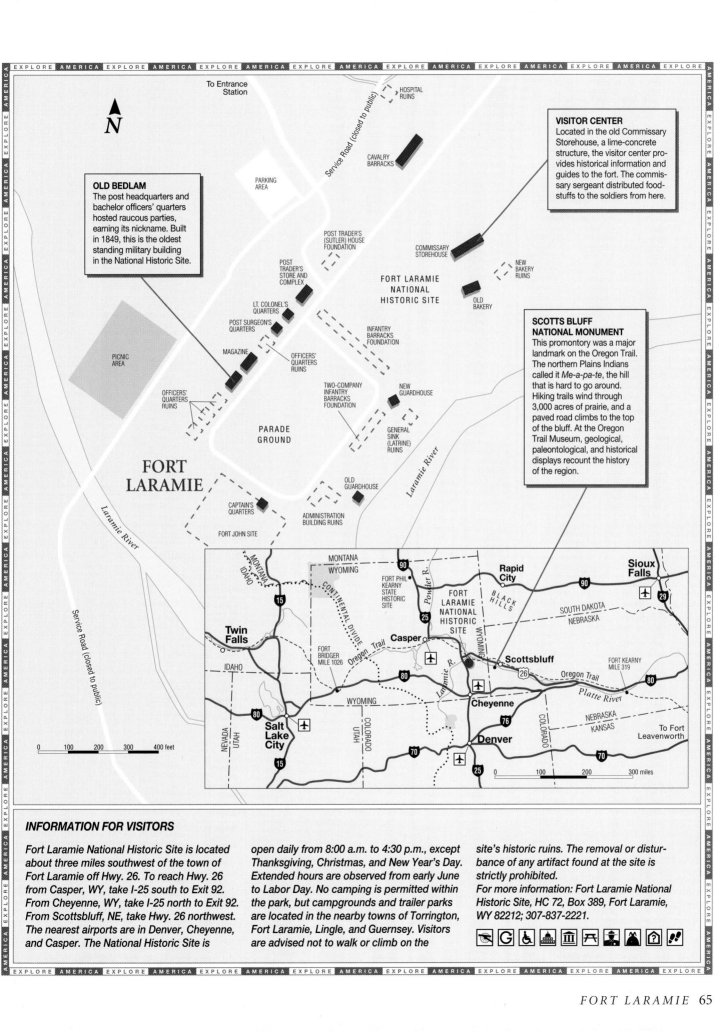

N

To Entrance Station

HOSPITAL RUINS

Service Road (closed to public)

CAVALRY BARRACKS

PARKING AREA

VISITOR CENTER
Located in the old Commissary Storehouse, a lime-concrete structure, the visitor center provides historical information and guides to the fort. The commissary sergeant distributed food-stuffs to the soldiers from here.

OLD BEDLAM
The post headquarters and bachelor officers' quarters hosted raucous parties, earning its nickname. Built in 1849, this is the oldest standing military building in the National Historic Site.

POST TRADER'S (SUTLER) HOUSE FOUNDATION

COMMISSARY STOREHOUSE

NEW BAKERY RUINS

OLD BAKERY

FORT LARAMIE NATIONAL HISTORIC SITE

POST TRADER'S STORE AND COMPLEX

LT. COLONEL'S QUARTERS

POST SURGEON'S QUARTERS

MAGAZINE

OFFICERS' QUARTERS RUINS

INFANTRY BARRACKS FOUNDATION

SCOTTS BLUFF NATIONAL MONUMENT
This promontory was a major landmark on the Oregon Trail. The northern Plains Indians called it *Me-a-pa-te*, the hill that is hard to go around. Hiking trails wind through 3,000 acres of prairie, and a paved road climbs to the top of the bluff. At the Oregon Trail Museum, geological, paleontological, and historical displays recount the history of the region.

PICNIC AREA

OFFICERS' QUARTERS RUINS

TWO-COMPANY INFANTRY BARRACKS FOUNDATION

NEW GUARDHOUSE

GENERAL SINK (LATRINE) RUINS

PARADE GROUND

Laramie River

FORT LARAMIE

OLD GUARDHOUSE

CAPTAIN'S QUARTERS

ADMINISTRATION BUILDING RUINS

FORT JOHN SITE

Laramie River

Service Road (closed to public)

0 100 200 300 400 feet

MONTANA / IDAHO

MONTANA / WYOMING

90

FORT PHIL KEARNEY STATE HISTORIC SITE

Powder R.

Rapid City

BLACK HILLS

90

Sioux Falls

29

15

CONTINENTAL DIVIDE

25

FORT LARAMIE NATIONAL HISTORIC SITE

SOUTH DAKOTA / NEBRASKA

Twin Falls

FORT BRIDGER MILE 1026

Oregon Trail

Casper

WYOMING

Scottsbluff

26

FORT KEARNY MILE 319

Oregon Trail

IDAHO

80

Laramie R.

Platte River

80

WYOMING

Cheyenne

NEBRASKA / KANSAS

To Fort Leavenworth

NEVADA / UTAH

COLORADO / UTAH

76

Denver

COLORADO

80

Salt Lake City

70

25

70

0 100 200 300 miles

INFORMATION FOR VISITORS

Fort Laramie National Historic Site is located about three miles southwest of the town of Fort Laramie off Hwy. 26. To reach Hwy. 26 from Casper, WY, take I-25 south to Exit 92. From Cheyenne, WY, take I-25 north to Exit 92. From Scottsbluff, NE, take Hwy. 26 northwest. The nearest airports are in Denver, Cheyenne, and Casper. The National Historic Site is open daily from 8:00 a.m. to 4:30 p.m., except Thanksgiving, Christmas, and New Year's Day. Extended hours are observed from early June to Labor Day. No camping is permitted within the park, but campgrounds and trailer parks are located in the nearby towns of Torrington, Fort Laramie, Lingle, and Guernsey. Visitors are advised not to walk or climb on the site's historic ruins. The removal or disturbance of any artifact found at the site is strictly prohibited.

For more information: Fort Laramie National Historic Site, HC 72, Box 389, Fort Laramie, WY 82212; 307-837-2221.

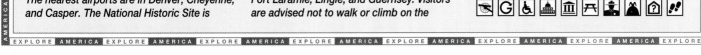

warring tribes kept their distance from each other. The allied tribes ate the food provided by the government and visited among the many lodges, and their leaders "touched the pen," or signed the treaty.

UNEASY PEACE

Government emissaries to the 1851 Fort Laramie Council proclaimed peace over the northern Plains, an announcement that was trumpeted by newspapers in the East. But nothing changed. The Lakota continued to make war on their enemies, and the Crow, Shoshoni, and Pawnee responded in kind. Government rations and goods—called annuities—were shipped westward as promised by the treaty. Some of the annuities were confiscated by corrupt Indian agents and others were refused by Lakota and Cheyenne leaders, who asserted that those who had touched the pen at Fort Laramie did not represent their people. These leaders wanted nothing to do with the white men who had encroached on their land—the most formidable enemy they had ever encountered. "You have split my land," declared a Lakota chief to officials at Fort Laramie, "and I don't like it."

Friction between the U.S. government and the Lakota nation reached a flashpoint at Fort Laramie. In 1853 a group of Miniconjou Lakota appropriated a ferryboat used by soldiers to transport emigrants. An angry sergeant took the craft back, and one of the Lakota fired a shot at him. Troops were ordered to search the nearby Miniconjou village and apprehend the shooter, but the Lakota insisted they would handle the matter themselves. The troops advanced and several Lakota fled, firing as they ran. Three Lakota were killed by return fire. Tensions brewed among the hundreds of Lakota camped by the fort, but they were temporarily eased by the Indian agent Thomas "Broken Hand" Fitzpatrick, a former mountain man whose even-handed negotiations soothed Lakota tempers.

Unfortunately, it was to be a short-lived peace. On August 19, 1854, a lame cow strayed from a wagon train of emigrants as they neared Fort Laramie and wandered into a nearby Lakota camp, where it was killed and butchered. When the emigrants reached Fort Laramie they reported the cow as stolen. The next day a brash young officer named Lieut. John Grattan led 29 men, armed with two cannons, to the Lakota camp to arrest the Indians who had slaughtered the cow. After negotiations stalled, a panicked soldier fired without orders at a group of Lakota. In the ensuing melee, a Lakota chief, Bear That Scatters His Enemies, as well as several Lakota warriors were killed. Grattan's entire command was cut down. The simmering tensions between the two factions had boiled over.

PRIVATE VIEW
The frame and adobe buildings that originally housed officers and their families were replaced in 1882 by lime-and-concrete structures, above.

summoning them to council. Rations and goods were offered to those who agreed to attend. The Pawnee flatly refused to go, but some tribal leaders among the Crow and Shoshoni decided to risk a meeting with the Lakota and they assembled at the fort. The Oglala Lakota were there in full force, and were joined by allies of the Brulé Lakota, Cheyenne, Arapaho, and other Indian nations. The

In retaliation for the death of Bear That Scatters His Enemies, a Lakota war party attacked a mail wagon, killing three teamsters. The following year the massacre of Grattan's command was avenged by 600 troops led by Brig. Gen. William S. Harney, ordered up from Fort Kearny in Nebraska.

At dawn on September 3, 1855, Harney's troops fell on a camp of Oglala and Brulé Lakota under Chief Little Thunder near Ash Hollow in North Platte country. Both sides attempted a truce and failed. Eighty-six Lakota were killed, 70 women and children were taken captive, and the camp was destroyed. Along with scalps of white women, Harney found articles from the mail wagon in the camp. He ordered the local Lakota tribes to surrender the mail wagon raiders to Fort Laramie or face further punishment. The Lakota complied and sent five young warriors into the post, dressed for battle and singing death songs. Taken to Fort Leavenworth, the group expected to be hanged. Instead, Pres. Franklin Pierce pardoned them in a goodwill gesture that profited the government in later years: one of the warriors became Chief Spotted Tail, a tireless advocate for peace.

Fear and hatred on the northern Plains were further aroused when more than 400 Minnesota settlers were killed in the 1862 Santee Sioux uprising. At Fort Laramie, a small garrison was surprised when a group of Lakota drove away a string of army horses from the parade ground. Bloodshed seemed inevitable, but Fort Laramie's experienced commander, the wise and fair Col. William O. Collins, managed to keep the peace.

News of the Minnesota massacres touched off other violence, and deadly Indian raids were met with harsh, sometimes barbaric, retaliation. In a punitive army campaign against the Lakota of the Powder River country northwest of Fort Laramie, soldiers burned an Arapaho village, but the troops were so harassed by Lakota warriors that they withdrew in a humiliating retreat.

In the 1860's gold was discovered in Montana and a new route to the goldfields, the Bozeman Trail, was cut from the North Platte above Fort Laramie to Virginia City. The government decided to negotiate peace treaties with the Indians at the same time that it was planning a series of new forts along the Bozeman Trail. Lakota leaders were invited to Fort Laramie in 1866, but when the Lakota learned of the plans for the new forts they saw no alternative but to resist. Led by Chief Red Cloud, the Lakota made repeated raids and attacks on Fort Phil Kearny on the Bozeman Trail. In December a Christmas ball at Fort Laramie was disrupted by the dramatic arrival of an army scout. He had ridden for four days through a blizzard to plead for reinforcements after Lakota warriors wiped out a troop of soldiers within earshot of the fort.

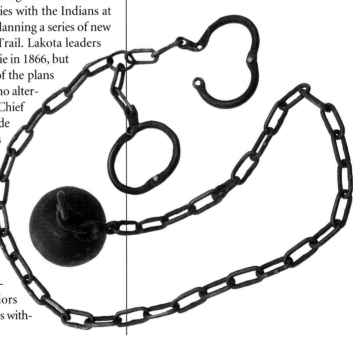

Red Cloud's War, as the Lakota resistance became known, was so effective that the government gave up the effort to defeat them. Indian commissioners were instructed in April 1868 to lure Lakota leaders to peace negotiations with piles of annuities. What emerged was the Fort Laramie Treaty, which promised to close the Bozeman Trail and abandon the posts. Red Cloud refused to sign, however, until the troops had left and his warriors had burned down the forts. It was the only war with the U.S. Army ever won by Indians.

An eight-year period of peace followed. Then, in 1874, the fragile truce began to crumble again when gold was found in the Black Hills of present-day South Dakota, northeast of Fort Laramie. The Lakota, who had won the Black Hills in bloody

WEARY HORSEMEN
Sixty cavalrymen slept side by side in the second-floor squad bay of the cavalry barracks, above. These volunteers, often recent immigrants to the United States, enlisted for a salary of about $13 a month. At Fort Laramie's peak in the 1870's, most cavalrymen were armed with .45 Colt revolvers or .45 calibre Springfield carbines (a single-shot breech loader). The soldiers were also issued sabers, but they rarely got close enough to the enemy to use them.

fighting with other tribes, refused to sell them now to white gold miners, who rushed into the region anyway. The prospectors set up makeshift towns like Deadwood and beseeched the army for protection. The Grant administration mulled over the matter, then ordered all Indians onto ceded land on reservations. When the Lakota ignored the demand, the army took action.

Fort Laramie was a major staging point for the later campaign against the Lakota. Troops from the fort joined one of the columns of soldiers sent to Yellowstone in 1876. Led by Gen. George Crook, the column was turned back by the Lakota under Crazy Horse at the Battle of the Rosebud on June 17, 1876. A week later another column, under Lieut. Col. George A. Custer, attacked an encampment of Lakota and Cheyenne on the Little Bighorn River in Montana. Custer and his immediate command of more than 250 men were wiped out in what would be the Lakota nation's greatest—and last—victory, the Battle of the Little Bighorn.

FORCIBLE REMOVAL

The response from the government was swift and decisive. Large numbers of soldiers ultimately defeated and dispersed the Sioux and Cheyenne, forcing them onto reservations. In 1890 the army shut down Fort Laramie. The American frontier was declared officially closed and the tumultuous events that had swirled around the great post on Wyoming's Laramie River receded into the pages of history.

MILITARY TOWN
The restored frame captain's quarters, left side of photo, and the bachelor officers' quarters, right side, at Fort Laramie National Historic Site, bracket the lime-and-concrete ruins of the officers' quarters. Between 1849 and 1885 the fort grew to include approximately 200 buildings. When General Sherman visited Fort Laramie in 1868 he described it as "a mixture of all sorts of houses of every conceivable pattern and promise."

NEARBY SITES & ATTRACTIONS

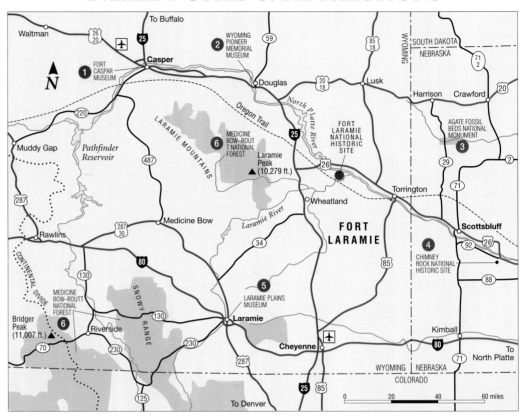

Pioneers relied on Chimney Rock, above, as a guide in the westward trek along the Oregon Trail. Many settlers set up camp near the spire to take advantage of the abundant fresh water supplied by the North Platte River.

① FORT CASPAR MUSEUM, WYOMING

The Wyoming plains were the traditional homelands of the Shoshoni, Cheyenne, Arapaho, and Lakota Indians. In the 1840's traders, settlers, and Mormons passed through this region on their way to settle the West. Trader Louis Guinard built the Platte Bridge Station in 1859, consisting of a trading post and tall bridge across the North Platte River. Later, the site included a stagecoach stop, Pony Express, and a telegraph office. When hostilities between northern Plains Indians and settlers broke out, U.S. troops were sent to the area. In 1865 the Cheyenne and Lakota tried to destroy the trading post and halt westward traffic. More than 1,000 Indians descended on the bridge, killing Lt. Caspar Collins. The army changed the name of the post to Fort Caspar in his honor. The fort was abandoned two years later, but local residents reconstructed it in 1936 based on sketches by Collins. Visitors can tour the log fort as well as the mess hall, telegraph office, and officers' quarters, all of which are furnished in period style. A museum displays exhibits relating to military life and the social and natural history of central Wyoming. Located at 4001 Fort Caspar Rd. in Casper.

② WYOMING PIONEER MEMORIAL MUSEUM, WYOMING

One of the primary goals of the Wyoming Pioneer Association when it was incorporated in 1926 was to acquire mementos and artifacts that predated statehood in 1890. As the collection grew, the association decided to open a museum, which now comprises four main galleries. On display in the Pioneer Gallery are saddles, firearms, homesteading tools, furniture, and items from several forts in Wyoming. The East Gallery exhibits clothing, dishes, and toys of the early 20th century and houses the museum's permanent art collection. The Johnson Gallery contains an extensive collection of Native American beadwork, basketry, and quillwork. The lower level displays farming and ranching tools and mining equipment. Books, photographs, and manuscripts are on view in the library. Located on the Wyoming State Fairgrounds in Douglas.

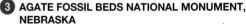

③ AGATE FOSSIL BEDS NATIONAL MONUMENT, NEBRASKA

Nineteen million years ago creatures such as the two-horned menoceras and the moropus—a clawed animal resembling a combination bear, giraffe, and horse—roamed the great plains of what is now Nebraska. The skeletons of these and other mammals were fossilized and deposited in two sandstone hills within the monument. A two-mile round-trip to view the exposed fossils begins at the visitor center, which also offers a museum that displays a life-size diorama of the ancient animals that once roamed the area. Several Lakota Indian artifacts connected with the site are also on display. Nature lovers can observe the park's abundant wildlife, which includes birds, deer, coyotes, raccoons, foxes, and badgers. Located 22 miles south of Harrison off Hwy. 29.

5 LARAMIE PLAINS MUSEUM, WYOMING

Once one of Laramie's grandest houses and listed on the National Register of Historic Places, the lavish Ivinson Mansion is now home to a museum that displays tools, cookware, furniture, clothing, and buggies dating from Wyoming's early pioneer days. The mansion was named after Edward Ivinson, who was born in St. Croix, Virgin Islands, and later emigrated to England and then to the United States. He erected the Queen Anne–style house in 1892. One of Laramie's prominent citizens, Ivinson served as its mayor at the age of 88. His wife, Jane, whom he married when she was 14, spearheaded local educational and church activities in the town. After her death in 1815, Ivinson deeded his mansion to the Episcopalian church, which turned it into a boarding school for girls. The school closed in 1958, and the beautiful house stood empty until it was opened as a museum in 1973. A tour of the house takes in the formal dining room, well-equipped kitchen, and a restored drawing room. Located at 603 Ivinson Ave. in Laramie.

6 MEDICINE BOW–ROUTT NATIONAL FOREST, COLORADO/WYOMING

Spread out over two states, the forest is composed of more than 3 million acres, and takes in several mountain ranges, many with summits that tower above 10,000 feet. The rugged Laramie Mountains include 10,272-foot Laramie Peak. To the west, the Sherman subrange is renowned for its unusual rock formations, created by erosion. The Medicine Bow Mountains are also known as the Snowy Range because of their outcroppings of white quartzite and their snowcapped peaks. The Continental Divide crosses the westernmost section of the forest. Douglas fir, aspen, and lodgepole pine flourish at lower levels, Engelmann spruce and subalpine fir grow at higher elevations, and wildflowers dot the high-country meadows in the summer. The mountains provide a habitat for elk, black bears, deer, bighorn sheep, and mountain lions. Located in southeastern Wyoming.

Cheyenne legend has it that the jumbled rock formations, left, in the Laramie mountain range were created by the playful spirits of men and animals.

4 CHIMNEY ROCK NATIONAL HISTORIC SITE, NEBRASKA

Towering 500 feet above the Nebraska plains, Chimney Rock signaled the end of the prairies and the beginning of the Rockies for immigrants traveling west along the Oregon Trail. It was first documented in 1813 by Robert Stuart and a band of traders. The column, which is composed of Brule clay, sandstone, and volcanic ash, has eroded a great deal during the past two centuries. The visitor center runs a short film on the landmark spire, and the Nebraska State Historical Society operates a display during the summer that focuses on the history and geology of the region. Animals in the area include golden eagles, hawks, deer, antelopes, and rattlesnakes. Located 25 miles southeast of Scottsbluff near the intersection of Hwys. 26 and 92.

Fort Caspar, left, operated as a military fort between 1861 and 1867. For the first three years the fort was a one-company military post. In 1865, when hostilities between the Plains Indians and the army erupted, the fort's complement of troops grew to include members of the 11th Ohio Volunteer Cavalry, the 11th Kansas Volunteer Cavalry, the 3rd U.S. Volunteer Infantry, and the 6th U.S. Volunteer Infantry.

FORT SUMTER

Built to guard Charleston from foreign attack, this fort was the site of the first battle in the Civil War.

From atop the heavy brick walls of Fort Sumter, Maj. Robert Anderson gazed upon Charleston in April 1861 the way many others had before him—over the barrel of a cannon. In 1670 English settlers had established the colony of Charles Towne in what is now South Carolina. Charleston, as the city is now called, had often been at the center of conflict. Fraught with Indian uprisings, Spanish invasion, slave revolts, pirate raids, British attacks, bombardments, sieges, fires, floods, hurricanes, and earthquakes, Charleston had always survived. Now, in the spring of 1861, the port city was facing its greatest crisis, one that would soon grip all of America.

Tensions between the North and South had smoldered for decades, with dangerous flare-ups occurring on many fronts. Looking to boost manufacturing in the more industrialized North, leaders in that part of the country sought to restrict foreign imports by imposing high tariffs. This action, in turn, alienated Southern farmers and planters, who relied heavily on imported goods to

survive. Progressive-minded Northerners favored a strong federal government, but most Southerners looked with suspicion on a centralized authority.

Tossed like volatile fuel on the flickering fire of civil tension was the issue of slavery. It was a nationwide institution—slavery was legal in New York for almost two centuries before it was abolished in 1827. The practice was allowed by the Constitution and upheld by the U.S. Supreme Court. Although less than 20 percent of Southerners owned slaves in 1860, slavery had come to symbolize the differences between the two cultures. Southerners, alarmed by John Brown's raid on Harpers Ferry in 1859, took a defensive posture, convinced that Northerners and their political leaders were determined to do the South harm. When the election of 1860 placed the White House under the control of the newly formed Republican Party—hated as anti-Southern by its critics—South Carolina officially seceded from the Union.

Other states followed South Carolina's example, and secessionists declared nationhood as the Confederate States of America. Southerners saw themselves as a new generation of Washingtons and Jeffersons whose proclamation of independence preserved the ideal of liberty from an oppressive federal government. On the other hand, many Northern leaders felt that secession must be quelled at any cost.

MOVING THE TROOPS

On December 26, 1860, Maj. Robert Anderson was the senior U.S. Army officer in command of abandoned Fort Johnson; unmanned Castle Pinckney; Fort Sumter, which was still under construction; and Fort Moultrie, with 50 guns and 80 or so officers. He surprised his troops with an abrupt order: be ready to move in 20 minutes. Six days earlier, South Carolina's legislature had voted to secede from the Union, and Anderson feared secessionists might try to capture his garrison. A 55-year-old career army officer, the major knew that Fort Moultrie, where his troops were posted, was practically indefensible: civilian houses looked over its walls, their roofs providing enemy sharpshooters with an easy target; it was weak on the land side; and Anderson's skeleton force was too small even to man all its guns. As nighttime cloaked Charleston Harbor and the city's lights began to glow, Major Anderson and his troops rowed through the dark waters until

they could make out the thick walls of Fort Sumter towering ahead of them.

Named for South Carolina Revolutionary War hero Gen. Thomas Sumter, the three-story masonry fort was still under construction. Even so, it enjoyed several advantages: it was sturdily built, surrounded by water, and had 135 guns that could provide heavy seacoast artillery when mounted. Built on a shoal overlooking Charleston's ship channel, Fort Sumter was a mighty fortress compared to the worn ramparts of Fort Moultrie.

To the surprise of a civilian construction crew, Anderson posted his troops around Fort Sumter and ordered his rear guard at Fort Moultrie to burn the seven gun carriages facing Fort Sumter, spike the remaining 43 guns, and chop down the post flagpole—unmistakable signs of an impending battle. Anderson had moved his troops to a secure post that they would defend to the end. Anderson considered his actions to be a military necessity. Officials of the newly formed Republic of South Carolina, however, did not agree. They viewed both the move and Anderson's methods as hostile.

Furthermore, they believed Fort Sumter rested on borrowed soil that belonged to the sovereign state of South Carolina. Just days earlier, in what they considered to be an exercise of constitutional rights, state leaders had declared their independence from the federal Union. While they might compensate the U.S. government for federal arms, equipment, and facilities, the South Carolinians had insisted that the federal troops be evacuated. Instead, they faced a military confrontation. The issue of states' rights versus federal authority, which had been debated long and loud by both North and South, was about to ignite in warfare at Fort Sumter. Southern dreams of unchallenged independence and Northern hopes for peaceful preservation of the Union vanished in the crisis. "Why did that green goose Anderson go into Fort Sumter?" fretted Southern diarist Mary Boykin Chestnut. "Then everything began to go wrong."

Both sides prepared for the worst. Anderson readied Fort Sumter for battle, and South Carolina's militia forces repaired Fort Moultrie's damaged artillery and ringed the harbor with batteries. Meanwhile, South Carolina governor Francis Pickens sent a request to the federal capital asking authorities to withdraw all military forces from Charleston. Instead, the outgoing president, James

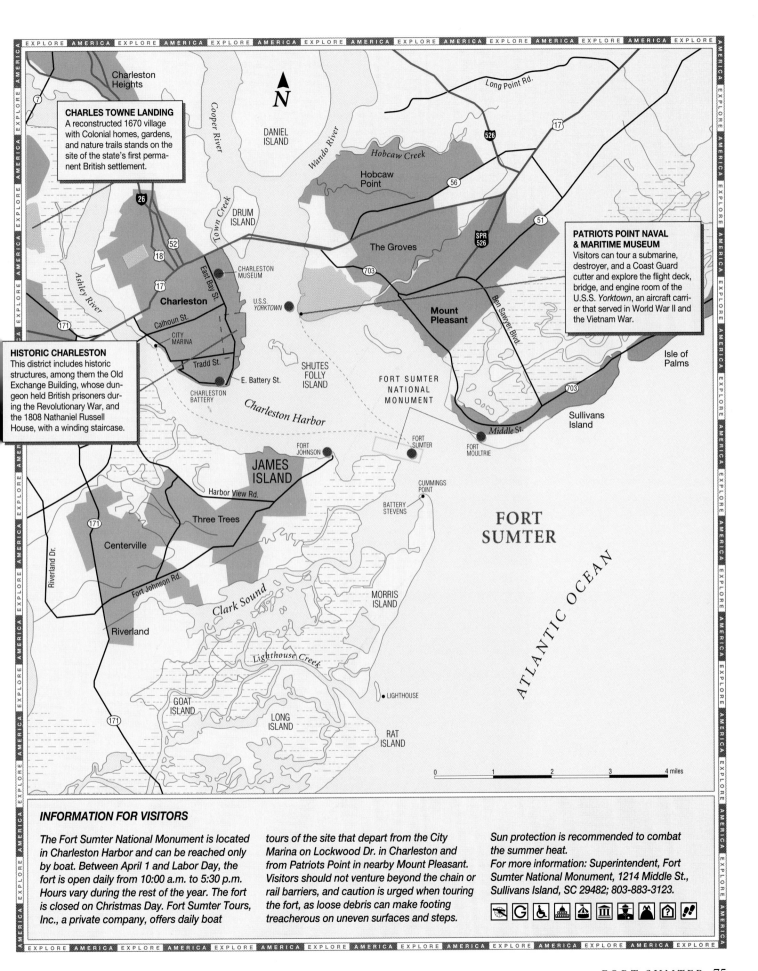

Charleston
Heights

⑦

N

CHARLES TOWNE LANDING
A reconstructed 1670 village
with Colonial homes, gardens,
and nature trails stands on the
site of the state's first permanent British settlement.

Cooper River

DANIEL
ISLAND

Wando River

Long Point Rd.

⑰

⑤②⑥

Hobcaw Creek

Hobcaw
Point

㊟

㊟

The Groves

㊞

②⑥

Town Creek

DRUM
ISLAND

SPR
526

51

CHARLESTON
MUSEUM

East Bay St.

⑱

⑤②

⑰

Charleston

Ashley River

⑰①

Calhoun St.

CITY
MARINA

Tradd St.

⑦⓪③

U.S.S.
YORKTOWN

**Mount
Pleasant**

Ben Sawyer Blvd.

**PATRIOTS POINT NAVAL
& MARITIME MUSEUM**
Visitors can tour a submarine,
destroyer, and a Coast Guard
cutter and explore the flight deck,
bridge, and engine room of the
U.S.S. *Yorktown,* an aircraft carrier that served in World War II and
the Vietnam War.

Isle of
Palms

HISTORIC CHARLESTON
This district includes historic
structures, among them the Old
Exchange Building, whose dungeon held British prisoners during the Revolutionary War, and
the 1808 Nathaniel Russell
House, with a winding staircase.

E. Battery St.

CHARLESTON
BATTERY

SHUTES
FOLLY
ISLAND

FORT SUMTER
NATIONAL
MONUMENT

Charleston Harbor

Sullivans
Island

Middle St.

FORT
SUMTER

FORT
MOULTRIE

FORT
JOHNSON

**JAMES
ISLAND**

Harbor View Rd.

CUMMINGS
POINT

BATTERY
STEVENS

**FORT
SUMTER**

Three Trees

⑰①

Centerville

Fort Johnson Rd.

MORRIS
ISLAND

Riverland Dr.

Clark Sound

ATLANTIC OCEAN

Riverland

Lighthouse Creek

• LIGHTHOUSE

GOAT
ISLAND

LONG
ISLAND

⑰①

RAT
ISLAND

0   1   2   3   4 miles

INFORMATION FOR VISITORS

*The Fort Sumter National Monument is located
in Charleston Harbor and can be reached only
by boat. Between April 1 and Labor Day, the
fort is open daily from 10:00 a.m. to 5:30 p.m.
Hours vary during the rest of the year. The fort
is closed on Christmas Day. Fort Sumter Tours,
Inc., a private company, offers daily boat*

*tours of the site that depart from the City
Marina on Lockwood Dr. in Charleston and
from Patriots Point in nearby Mount Pleasant.
Visitors should not venture beyond the chain or
rail barriers, and caution is urged when touring
the fort, as loose debris can make footing
treacherous on uneven surfaces and steps.*

*Sun protection is recommended to combat
the summer heat.*
*For more information: Superintendent, Fort
Sumter National Monument, 1214 Middle St.,
Sullivans Island, SC 29482; 803-883-3123.*

Buchanan, sent an unarmed merchant ship, the *Star of the West,* to Charleston with 200 troops and provisions to resupply Fort Sumter's garrison. Buchanan's move provoked the South Carolina leaders. When the supply ship tried to enter Charleston Harbor on January 9, 1861, South Carolinian troops shot at the ship and it turned back. The first shot, reputedly fired by Citadel cadet George E. Haynsworth, is sometimes called the opening shot of the Civil War.

Anderson's men watched their supply ship being driven off and itched to return fire, but the orders from Washington required them to remain "strictly on the defensive." Anderson, a formal and reserved man, was now the central figure in a tense national crisis—a position he did not relish.

Following this initial confrontation, the test of nerves resumed, but by mid-March there were new players directing the events. Abraham Lincoln had succeeded Buchanan as president. Untested and holding office by a plurality, Lincoln was unable to command widespread confidence in the North: he had held only one term as a U.S. congressman and was not yet a household name. In Charleston, Governor Pickens had handed control of the crisis to the newly formed Confederate States of America. Brigadier General P. G. T. Beauregard, a highly regarded army engineer who had held the post of superintendent of West Point, was put in command of Southern forces in Charleston by Confederate president Jefferson Davis. By a twist of fate, during his days as a cadet in the late 1830's, Beauregard had received instruction from Major Anderson—who now faced him from just across the harbor at Fort Sumter. Though Beauregard and Anderson were the commanding officers in the crisis, the shots would be called by President Davis from the Confederate capital of Montgomery and by Lincoln from the White House.

In exchange for a peaceful transfer of Fort Sumter, the Confederate Congress offered the federal government unrestricted navigation of the southern end of the Mississippi River. But Lincoln rejected any official negotiations and declined to meet with a peace commission dispatched to Washington by the Confederate government. Lincoln argued that by holding discussions with Confederate officials, he would undermine his position that the seceded Southern states still belonged to the Union and were under federal authority. It was a view that he articulated in his inaugural speech, when he swore to "hold, occupy and possess" all property claimed by the federal government. However, the first time he had polled his cabinet, the sentiment was overwhelmingly in favor of giving up Fort Sumter.

INTERNAL OPPOSITION

Chief among Lincoln's critics was his own secretary of state, William H. Seward, who had pegged the president as an inept amateur in need of guidance by a seasoned hand. In the midst of the standoff, Seward independently opened negotiations with Southern leaders through an acquaintance, former U.S. Supreme Court justice John A. Campbell. In what appears to have been a well-intentioned attempt to assist the inexperienced Lincoln, Seward allowed Campbell, an Alabamian, to assure Davis and the Confederate cabinet that the Lincoln administration intended to evacuate Fort Sumter.

Lincoln did appear to waver. He openly considered a proposal to abandon the fort if Virginia agreed to remain in the Union. "A state for a fort is not bad business," he admitted. He kept his

options open, however, by ordering that a flotilla of federal warships be placed on standby in the event that it became necessary to mount an expedition to forcibly resupply the fort.

In late March, Lincoln sent three emissaries to Charleston. One was Capt. Gustavus W. Fox, a well-connected naval officer who had urged Buchanan and Lincoln to resupply Fort Sumter at all costs. Fox met with Governor Pickens and wrangled a visit to the fort, where he spoke with Anderson and secretly picked a spot for a troop landing. Lincoln's close friend Ward Lamon, another of the emissaries, also met with Pickens. Introducing himself as the president's confidential agent, Lamon spent much of his time discussing the logistics of evacuating Fort Sumter. By the time Lamon left, Pickens was convinced that Lincoln was going to back down and relinquish the fort.

Lincoln's third emissary, Stephen Hurlbut, a lawyer born in South Carolina, returned to Washington with the gloomy news that the South Carolinians would resist federal authority and would never freely return to the Union—regardless of what happened to Fort Sumter.

Lincoln took action on April 6: he ordered a naval expedition to resupply the fort. When word of these intentions reached Davis in Montgomery, he demanded an explanation from Secretary of State

Seward. Seward tried to assuage the Southern fears. "Faith as to Sumter fully kept," he assured the Confederates in writing. "Wait and see." On April 8, a White House envoy delivered an official presidential message to the governor of South Carolina: "I am directed by the President of the United States to notify you to expect an attempt will be made to supply Fort Sumter with provisions only." Do nothing to interfere with the reprovisioning, the governor was instructed, and no attempt would be made to reinforce the fort with troops or arms.

Davis and his advisers felt betrayed. After being told by Seward that Lincoln would abandon the fort, they learned instead that he was sending warships to resupply it. They felt they were being maneuvered into either repudiating the doctrine of state sovereignty at the heart of the quest for Southern independence, or firing the first shot in a war many Northerners and Southerners had tried so long to avoid. With time running out President Davis polled his advisers: should they back down, or willingly initiate a civil war?

Confederate secretary of state Robert Tombs, a former U.S. senator from Georgia, warned Davis, "at this time it is suicide, murder, and you will lose us every friend in the North. You will wantonly strike a hornet's nest which extends from mountains to ocean. Legions now quiet will swarm out

OUT OF ITS ELEMENT
A replica of the H. L. Hunley, *a Confederate submarine, above, is named for its designer, Capt. Horace Lawson Hunley. The submarine is on display at the Charleston Museum. Founded in 1773, the museum houses many Civil War artifacts, including a number that relate to the history of Fort Sumter. The museum is reputed to be America's first.*

WEAPONS OF WAR
The muskets shown above, an 1855 rifle musket, top, and the Sharps rifle, bottom, developed in 1859, were used extensively by soldiers of both sides during the war. The rifle musket weighed about 10 pounds.

and sting us to death." In a sense, Davis' decision was inevitable. He had been elected to lead an independent South—the world's newest democracy—and it was time, he believed, either to back down or to put up a fight. He issued orders to Beauregard in Charleston: demand the evacuation of the fort, and if refused, "reduce" Fort Sumter before federal warships arrive.

A politely worded but clear ultimatum was rowed across Charleston Harbor under a fluttering flag of truce. Anderson and his command would be transported "with company arms and property, and all private property" to any Northern military post they chose. The offer included another conciliatory gesture. "The flag which you have upheld so long and with so much fortitude, under the most trying circumstances," Anderson was assured, "may be saluted by you on taking it down." Anderson left the two Confederate emissaries waiting for 45 minutes as he pondered this missive in private. Then he handed them a written refusal. As the messengers prepared to leave, Anderson added a provocative admission. "Gentlemen," he told the officers, "if you do not batter the fort to pieces about us, we shall be starved out in a few days."

Beauregard promptly telegraphed Montgomery to advise President Davis both of Anderson's refusal and his parting comment. A last-minute attempt at negotiations was sent in return: "If Major Anderson will state the time at which, as indicated by him, he will evacuate, and agree that in the meantime he will not use his guns against us, unless ours should be employed against Fort Sumter, you are authorized thus to avoid the effusion of blood." Davis' response reached Fort Sumter at 12:45 a.m. on April 12, by which time the advance warships of Lincoln's expedition had already arrived off the shore of Charleston. The Confederate delegation knew that time was running out. Again Anderson was slow in replying: the Confederate officers waited impatiently for two and a half hours.

For almost four months Anderson had received ambiguous and contradictory directives from his superiors, being ordered neither to evacuate nor stand and fight. Beauregard knew that supply ships were on the way to Fort Sumter, a vital piece of information that Anderson was not aware of. When Beauregard ordered Anderson to surrender, he finally replied at 3:15 a.m. that he would evacuate on April 15—provided he did not receive either

CHANGING OF THE GUARD
Union gunners man the 100-pound Parrott rifle cannons at Battery Stevens on Morris Island, right, in 1863. Two years earlier, the battery had been used by Confederate troops to bombard Fort Sumter.

orders to the contrary or fresh supplies. But with federal warships already arriving, it was the Confederates who had to back down or decide to bombard the fort. Anderson, a religious and patriotic man who wanted to avoid bloodshed, shook hands with Confederate officers. "If we never meet in this world again," he told the Southerners, "God grant that we may meet in the next."

| THE BATTLE BEGINS | At 4:30 a.m. on April 12, 1861, Capt. George S. James fired a signal gun from Confederate-held Fort Johnson, located on |

James Island, due west of Fort Sumter. A 10-inch mortar shell, trailing bright sparks from its burning fuse, arced through the morning darkness above Charleston Harbor and exploded right over the fort. Within seconds, the Confederate batteries that ringed the harbor opened fire and unleashed a thunderous bombardment on Fort Sumter.

Beauregard's Confederate artillery quickly found the fort's range and pounded its masonry walls. Inside Fort Sumter were Anderson; 5 headquarters' staff; 32 men from Company E, 1st U.S. Artillery; 32 men from Company H, 1st U.S. Artillery; 8 members of the regimental band; 1 member of the hospital staff; and 40 pro-Union civilian workmen who agreed to remain inside to strengthen the fort's defenses. Restricted by limited ammunition, Anderson issued orders to return fire at daylight—but no more than once every 10 minutes. It was almost 7:00 a.m. when the fort first returned fire. Captain Abner Doubleday, often credited with the invention of baseball, was Anderson's senior officer and fired Fort Sumter's opening shot, using a 32-pounder that was directed at Stevens Ironclad Battery on Morris Island. The shot bounced off the battery's plating without inflicting damage, but at least Fort Sumter was fighting back.

Anderson had propped up one of his most powerful guns so that its fire could reach Charleston's civilian neighborhoods, but while federal artillery regularly bombarded city neighborhoods later in the war, Anderson limited his fire to military targets. One time, however, Doubleday turned his guns on noncombatants, aiming a round at a seaside hotel on Sullivans Island. The crowd that had gathered to watch the action scattered. One of Anderson's noncommissioned officers, Sgt. John Carmody, disobeyed orders and climbed to Fort Sumter's upper tier, where a row of heavy guns was charged and at the ready. One by one, Carmody discharged the huge weapons.

By the morning of April 13, fires were burning inside Fort Sumter, ammunition was dangerously low, the barracks were ablaze, and the magazine

damaged. Smoke wafted through the casemates, forcing most of the men to abandon their guns and lie facedown, breathing through wet handkerchiefs. At 12:45 that afternoon, Fort Sumter's flagstaff was shot down. Before it could be raised again, one of Beauregard's aides, former U.S. senator Louis T. Wigfall of Texas, who had resigned and moved to South Carolina, commandeered a rowboat and ordered the crew to take him to Fort Sumter. Wigfall was not authorized to make contact with the fort's defenders, but with smoke billowing from the fort, he imagined an awful slaughter inside and acted impulsively. Federal soldiers were

SOUTHERN SPLENDOR
A house on Charleston's East Battery Street, above, displays a two-story Charleston piazza, or porch. Lined up along the waterfront, the houses provided residents with spectacular views of the Confederate siege of Fort Sumter.

startled to see Wigfall appear at an embrasure in the smoke-filled fort, raising a white flag on the point of a sword. Wigfall confronted one of Anderson's officers and implored him to surrender. When the officer refused, Wigfall stomped to an open embrasure and vigorously waved his own white flag. One by one the Confederate batteries ceased firing on the fort.

At that moment, a soiled and soot-stained Anderson arrived on the scene, only to be asked by Wigfall to surrender. "I have already stated my terms for evacuation to General Beauregard," Anderson firmly replied, but he added a concession: "Instead of the 15th, I will go now."

MAKESHIFT AGREEMENT Believing that the white flag he had seen at the fort was flown by his opponents, Beauregard dispatched a boat with three aides to the fort. When the Confederates landed, they were surprised to find Wigfall, who had single-handedly negotiated an end to the fighting. When Anderson learned that Wigfall lacked the authority to make terms, the battle almost resumed. Instead, a makeshift agreement was entered into by both sides. At 1:30 p.m. on April 13, the bombardment ended. Nobody on either side had been killed. A single death occurred the next day as the fort was officially surrendered: when Anderson attempted to fire a 100-gun salute to his flag, the blank powder charge went off prematurely on the 15th round and the blast killed Pvt. Daniel Hough. The soldier was the first of more than 620,000 Americans who died in the next four years before the Civil War was over.

Immediately after Anderson and his troops departed, Confederate forces took possession of Fort Sumter. Throughout the bloody warfare that followed, Southern forces determinedly held on to the fort as an affirmation of both states' rights and Southern independence. Not until the last months of the war was the city of Charleston evacuated by Confederate forces and Fort Sumter conceded. At the war's end on April 14, 1865, Anderson, by then promoted to brigadier general, once again raised his flag above the battered fort in a symbolic Northern

BATTLE IN THE BAY
Flashes of cannonfire illuminate Charleston Harbor during the ill-fated Union effort to regain the Confederate stronghold in 1863, below. Five of the nine federal armored ships that joined in the offensive were disabled by the relentless bombardments launched from forts Sumter, Moultrie, Johnson, Battery Gregg, and other installations that could bear on the ships. After two and a half hours of fighting, the Union fleet was forced to abandon the assault.

PUBLISHED BY CURRIER & IVES.
BATTERY BEE.
CUMMINGS POINT.
FORT SUMTER.
NEW IRONSIDES.
FORT MOULTRIE.
152 NASSAU ST NEW YORK.

THE GREAT FIGHT AT CHARLESTON S.C. APRIL, 7TH 1863

*Between 9 United States 'Iron-Clads', under the command of Admiral Dupont; and Forts Sumter, Moultrie, and the Cummings Point Batteries in possession of the Rebels.—
The Iron-Clads carried only 32 Guns, while the Rebel Forts mounted over 300 of the heaviest calibre, but notwithstanding the great odds, the little Iron-clads went bravely into the fight, and for nearly two hours were under the most terrible fire ever witnessed on this earth, but being unable to reach Charleston on account of obstructions in the harbor, the Admiral reluctantly gave the order for the battle to cease, and the fleet to retire from the unequal contest.— The Keokuk was the only Iron-clad disabled in the fight.*

Doubling the irony, South Carolina transferred Fort Moultrie in 1960 to the National Park Service. Today Fort Moultrie is the federal headquarters for Fort Sumter. A visitor center provides an interpretive history of Fort Moultrie, displays artifacts, and provides a 20-minute orientation film. Visitors who tour the fort will be rewarded with additional perspectives on the conflict and a good view of Fort Sumter.

Fort Johnson, erected by the British in 1706 on the opposite side of the harbor, is where the war's first shot was fired. Visitors to the island can learn a little more about the battle. The fort, which primarily houses state offices today, is accessible by driving across James Island. None of the 1861 earthworks remain, and the place where Fort Johnson's signal gun was fired has eroded into the harbor. Civil War earthworks dating from circa 1863 and a powder magazine from the War of 1812 are described by interpretive signs.

Another related site is Charleston's Battery, located at the tip of the old city peninsula and so named for an artillery battery erected there during the War

COMBUSTIBLE CHAMBER
Reconstructed to look as it did in the mid-1800's, the powder magazine at Fort Moultrie, left, gives visitors a sense of how vulnerable the garrison was. The smallest spark might ignite the entire room.

victory celebration. Today the banners of both sides that took part in the Civil War flutter in the coastal breeze above Fort Sumter as symbols of a shared American tragedy.

Fort Sumter now sits dark and squat in the middle of Charleston Harbor. On regularly scheduled concession boats, visitors ferried to the site find a fort that is very different from the one Anderson and his men had defended so courageously. The 1861 pounding by Confederate batteries was just the beginning of Fort Sumter's ordeal: By war's end Union forces had landed more than 7 million pounds of shot and shell on the masonry structure, reducing most of it to rubble. For more than 80 years after the war, the fort remained a military post, altered and updated along the way, until it was deactivated by the army and transferred to the National Park Service in 1948.

The park museum interprets the siege and provides a contemporary overview of the Civil War era. On display is the storm flag that flew over the fort in 1861 and the first Southern flag raised at the contested fortress, as well as selected artifacts of the period. Unexploded artillery shells, embedded in the masonry in several places, testify to the battering the fort received in the Civil War. Preserved casemates house artillery.

Across the harbor on Sullivans Island, reached from Charleston via the landmark suspension span of the Cooper River Bridge, lies Fort Moultrie. Like Fort Sumter, this post was in use until after World War II, when, ironically, the U.S. Army deactivated and transferred it to the state of South Carolina.

of 1812. On the eve of the War Between the States —called the War for Southern Independence by some Charlestonians—the battery was a favorite local spot for strolls and picnics. Today tourists amble among the huge Civil War artillery pieces preserved there, sit beneath the palmetto and live oak trees, or stand on the sea wall and peer across the harbor at the sturdy form of Fort Sumter.

The structure bespeaks those days when it was the most hotly contested fort in the country. From its ramparts visitors can almost feel the ripples of the cataclysmic violence that once shook its walls— and the foundations of an entire nation.

VERY DIFFERENT VESSELS
A summer tour boat sidles up to the enormous aircraft carrier U.S.S. Yorktown, above, near Patriots Point in Charleston Harbor.

A graceful staircase sweeps to the front door of Savannah's Davenport House, above. The house is a quintessential example of Federal-style architecture. Its interior is decorated to reflect the lifestyle of a middle-class family of the 1820's.

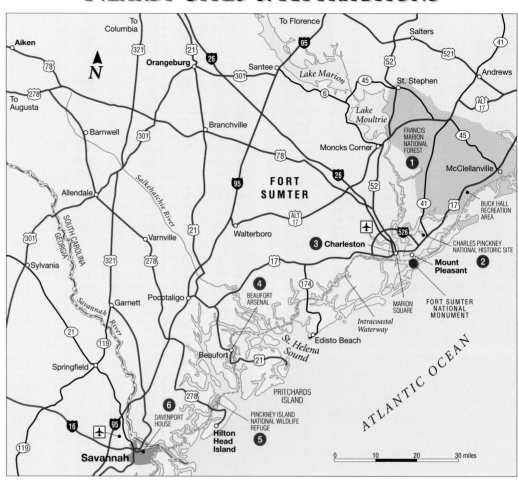

1 FRANCIS MARION NATIONAL FOREST, SOUTH CAROLINA

Inky swamps, low flatlands, and huge, moss-covered oaks dominate this 250,000-acre forest. Its many small lakes, called Carolina Bays, are thought to have been gouged out of the earth by meteors. The site was occupied by Native Americans for about 10,000 years before it was settled by French Huguenots in the late 1600's. The Revolutionary War general Francis Marion took refuge in the region's swamps after battling the British, earning himself the nickname Swamp Fox. Stands of longleaf pine invite exploration, and the limestone outcroppings lining Dutart Creek draw the eye. Campsites within the national forest range from very primitive to modern. Buck Hall Recreation Area, which overlooks the Cape Romain National Wildlife Refuge, includes 14 campsites. Pitch and Price landings in the Wambaw Ranger District offer boat launches for canoes and other small craft. Located northeast of Charleston off Hwys. 52 and 17.

2 CHARLES PINCKNEY NATIONAL HISTORIC SITE, SOUTH CAROLINA

This museum is housed in one of the few remaining Low Country cottages that were once common to the region. Several displays in the 1828 cottage are devoted to Charles Pinckney, who, although he never lived there, is remembered for his significant role in framing the U.S. Constitution. The museum also covers Pinckney's career as an elected official. He served as the governor of South Carolina and a member of the House of Representatives and of the Senate. Exhibits provide insights into the area's agricultural and social history, including the impact and influence of slavery. Archeological finds uncovered in the region are on display. Located six miles northeast of Charleston on Hwy. 17.

3 CHARLESTON, SOUTH CAROLINA

Despite 300 years of war, fire, earthquakes, and hurricanes, much of Charleston's beautiful architecture has been saved. The city council has set aside 233 blocks as an architectural preserve. The historic district, which is best enjoyed on foot, includes more than 1,000 historic structures, 73 of them dating to the late 17th century. Many examples of fine ornamental wrought iron by the 20th-century African-American artist Philip Simmons adorn homes here. The Aiken-Rhett Mansion on Elizabeth Street boasts rooms in the Federal style, and was used as the headquarters for Confederate general P. G. T. Beauregard during the Civil War. The Old Citadel building on Hampton Park, which now houses the famous military school called The Citadel, was built in 1822 on Marion Square and later moved to its present location. The Unitarian Church on Archdale Street was built in the late 1700's, making it the oldest Unitarian church in the South. In the 1850's builders added Gothic Revival touches to the church, including pointed arches and a vaulted ceiling. On Cabbage Row, off Church Street, stands Heyward-Washington House, where DuBose Heyward wrote the novel *Porgy,* the inspiration for the Gershwin operetta *Porgy and Bess,* America's first opera. From mid-March to mid-April the Historic Charleston Foundation holds a popular festival of houses that includes symphony galas, oyster roasts, and candle-light tours of the city's fine homes.

4 BEAUFORT ARSENAL, SOUTH CAROLINA

If the walls of this venerable building could talk, they would tell a story of wars, triumphs, and survival. One of the nation's oldest arsenals, Beaufort was built in 1798 at the head of one of the largest natural harbors on the Atlantic Coast. The arsenal's original walls were concrete made of lime produced from burned oyster shells then mixed with sand and crushed oyster shells. In the 1850's, when the town of Beaufort was the seat of the secessionist move-ment, wealthy citizens donated money to rebuild the old arsenal. It was redone in Gothic Revival style with pointed arched windows, parapets, and a masonry facade. In December 1861 the Union forces occu-pied the town and the arsenal became the property of the U.S. Army. For the remainder of the war, the arsenal was used by Union troops to store military supplies. Because Beaufort was held by the North, the town's buildings were spared. A 1907 fire destroyed 40 buildings and circled the arsenal, which survived virtually unscathed. Renovations and addi-tions were made to the arsenal in the late 1930's, when it became the Beaufort Museum. The museum now displays permanent and rotating exhibits featur-ing various aspects of life and culture in Beaufort. Located at 713 Craven St. in Beaufort.

5 PINCKNEY ISLAND NATIONAL WILDLIFE REFUGE, SOUTH CAROLINA

These 4,053 acres, which include five freshwater ponds, salt marshes, five islands, and several small hammocks, were donated to the government as a wildlife refuge in 1975. Pinckney Island, the refuge's largest island, is so slender that, in many places, only a few feet of road separate the tidewaters on either side of the island. Four endangered species are found here: the wood stork, Southern bald eagle, peregrine falcon, and the American alligator. More than 14 miles of trails are available for hiking or bicy-cling, and motorized vehicles are forbidden inside the park. Visitors will notice the charred trunks of pine trees throughout the refuge. A program of pre-scribed burning, similar to the practice of some Native American tribes, is carried out during the winter months to rid the woods of dead trees, unde-sirable hardwoods, and other organic matter. The ashes produced in the burning offer the additional benefit of enriching the soil. Located about 10 miles north of Hilton Head Island off Hwy. 278.

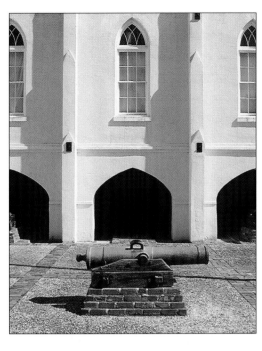

The Beaufort Museum is housed in the Beaufort Arsenal, left. Its collection covers a wide range of subjects related to the area's natural history and its military history.

6 DAVENPORT HOUSE, GEORGIA

Isaiah Davenport was a master builder from Rhode Island who came to Savannah to take advantage of the building boom spurred by a disastrous fire in 1796 that destroyed much of the city. He built this Federal-style home for his family in 1820. When the house was slated to be demolished in 1955, a group of seven women raised the $22,500 needed to buy it. The group went on to establish the nonprofit Historic Savannah Foundation. Located at 324 East State St. in Savannah.

Wild turkeys, deer, raccoons, and alligators live among the cypress and oak trees in the Wambaw Swamp Wilderness, below, at the Francis Marion National Forest.

SIEGE OF VICKSBURG

A 47-day siege, backed by a massive Union bombardment, brought the town of Vicksburg to its knees.

The cannons on the grassy bluff above Vicksburg still point toward the Mississippi River. These old Civil War batteries, known as Louisiana Circle and South Fort, were once considered insurmountable. Below their barrels the wide swath of the river takes a hairpin turn, at an angle that forced riverboats to reduce speed just as they came into artillery range. Today highway and railroad bridges and the neon lights of floating casinos are visible through the gun sights. But although the years have redrawn the landscape, it is still starkly evident as to why, in the early 1860's, Vicksburg was known as the Gibraltar of the Confederacy. More than a century ago, military wisdom held that not even the most heavily armed navy flotilla could break through these mighty defenses without being blown asunder by the ferocious cannon fire.

From Cairo, Illinois, to its bird's-foot delta south of New Orleans, the Mississippi twists across 1,000 miles of alluvial plain. Its banks offer little in the way of geography that could give

STANDING GUARD
Overleaf: A line of 20 antique cannons marks the site of DeGolyer's 8th Michigan Battery on the Union line. Behind the battery stands the 37-foot Michigan Monument and its symbol of the Spirit of Michigan, a female figure offering laurels to the soldiers of that state who fought in the Vicksburg campaign.

MODERN VIEW
Battery Benton at Navy Circle, below, west of Vicksburg on Warrenton Road, affords a picture-perfect view of the Mississippi River Bridges at sunset. Navy Circle marked the southern anchor of the Union lines.

land-based troops superiority over enemy warships and still protect them from an overland assault.

Except at Vicksburg, the river slices along the western edge of an escarpment that angles south-easterly from southern Kentucky, across Tennessee, and down to Baton Rouge. Vicksburg sits on the Walnut Hills in Mississippi. In 1863 the land to the north and south of it was mostly snake- and mosquito-infested swamp with myriad rivers, creeks, and bayous that were subject to frequent flooding. Ravines and dense undergrowth to the east were nearly as difficult to penetrate.

FORMIDABLE CITY

Whoever held Vicksburg held the Mississippi River—and without the Mississippi, a Union victory seemed impossible. Control of the artery would enable the Union to transport men and armaments to the South. With the river under Union jurisdiction, the Confederacy would be cut almost in half, isolating Texas, Arkansas, and much of Louisiana west of the river, thus drying up critical sources of supplies and manpower for the rebel cause.

Early in the war, the Confederate army had built fortifications along the river. But one by one the forts had fallen to Union troops as they advanced southward from Illinois and northward from the Gulf of Mexico. By the autumn of 1862 only two sites on the river—Vicksburg and Port Hudson in Louisiana, 200 miles to the south—remained in

BULL'S-EYE
As many as 22 Federal artillery pieces were positioned in Battery DeGolyer, above, their fire directed at the Great Redoubt, a defensive fortification constructed on the Confederate line.

INFORMATION FOR VISITORS

Vicksburg is located on I-20 between Monroe, LA, and Jackson, MS. The nearest commercial airport is found in Jackson, and Vicksburg is served by a municipal airport. The Vicksburg National Military Park offers an 18-minute film on the siege. A 16-mile driving tour, with numerous interpretive markers, begins at the visitor center. Picnicking is permitted on the grounds of the U.S.S. Cairo Museum and near the Second Texas Lunette, tour stop 12. There are no campsites within the park. The park is open year-round from 8:00 a.m. to 5:00 p.m., except Christmas Day.
For more information: Vicksburg National Military Park, 3201 Clay St., Vicksburg, MS 39180; 601-636-0583.
Vicksburg Convention and Visitors Bureau, P.O. Box 110, Vicksburg, MS 39181-0110; 601-636-9421 or 800-221-3536.

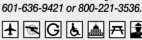

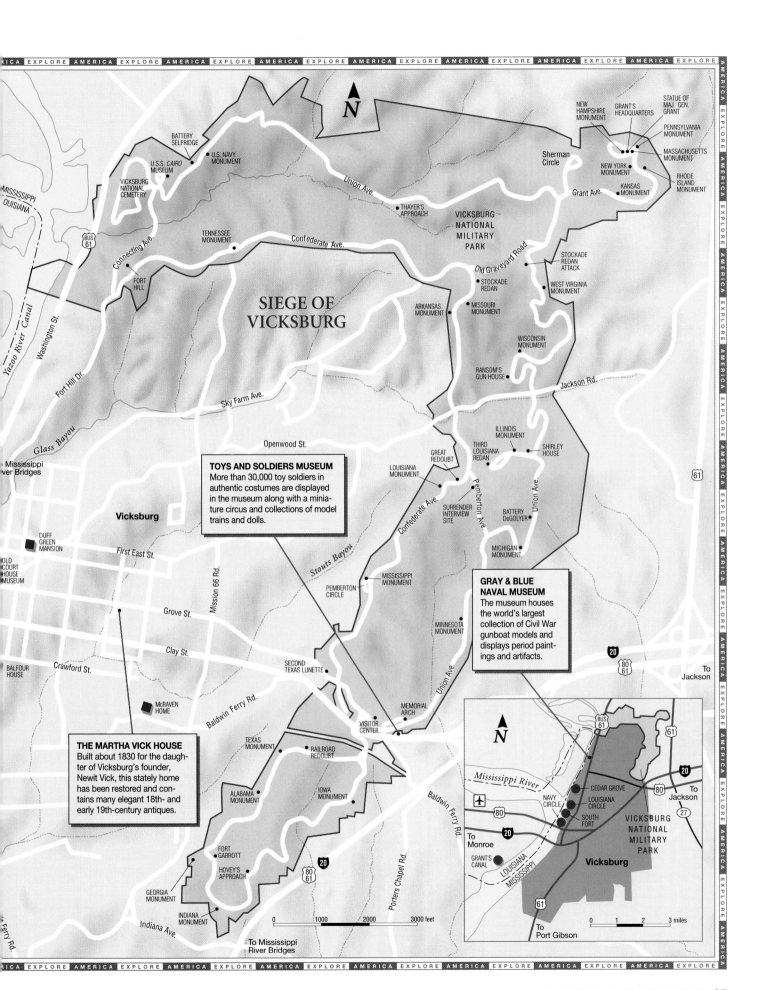

SIEGE OF VICKSBURG

TOYS AND SOLDIERS MUSEUM
More than 30,000 toy soldiers in authentic costumes are displayed in the museum along with a miniature circus and collections of model trains and dolls.

GRAY & BLUE NAVAL MUSEUM
The museum houses the world's largest collection of Civil War gunboat models and displays period paintings and artifacts.

THE MARTHA VICK HOUSE
Built about 1830 for the daughter of Vicksburg's founder, Newit Vick, this stately home has been restored and contains many elegant 18th- and early 19th-century antiques.

ICA EXPLORE AMERICA EXPLORE AMERICA EXPLORE AMERICA EXPLORE AMERICA EXPLORE AMERICA EXPLORE AMERICA EXPLORE AMERICA EXPLORE

SIEGE OF VICKSBURG 87

The imposing domed Illinois Monument, right, in Vicksburg National Military Park, is inscribed with the names of all of the participants in the battle from that state, including Fred Grant, the 12-year-old son of the victorious general, Ulysses S. Grant. Shirley House, seen to the right of the monument, was taken over by the 45th Illinois Infantry and converted into regimental headquarters.

BURNISHED GRASSES
Feathery wild millet, above, is wafted by gentle breezes in a field outside Vicksburg.

Confederate hands. Vicksburg was, by far, the most valuable strategic location.

As the war raged on and Confederate soldiers penetrated deeper into the entire length of Union territory, command of the Mississippi became more urgent. "Vicksburg is the key," Pres. Abraham Lincoln told his cabinet. "The war can never be brought to a close until that key is in our pocket."

NATIONAL MILITARY PARK

The bluffs overlooking the Mississippi River where the old battery sites stand are protected within several units of the Vicksburg National Military Park. Besides the howitzers in the park there are 8-inch Columbiads, 42-pound rifled guns, and a sleek little 7.44-inch weapon known as the Widow Blakely (one of the few artillery pieces that can be positively identified as having been employed in the conflict). The battle over who would control the city was fought along a boomerang-shaped arc that swings out from the river and around the town. This eight-mile line of gun positions, rifle pits, and sturdy forts held the Union army, under Gen. Ulysses S. Grant, at bay for six weeks.

Most of the arc lies within the 1,800 acres of the military park. From here it is easy for visitors to trace the progress of the siege on a tour that follows the movements of both armies. These are marked by trenches, earthworks, and natural land features that constituted the armies' battle lines.

Twenty-eight states sent soldiers to fight in this pivotal battle and all but one, Kentucky, have erected monuments, statues, and markers that identify the ground held by their native sons. The memorials resemble magnificent tombstones scattered beside the 16-mile roadway that follows the Union line up one side of the park and the Confederate troop position down the other.

The shaded tiers of lawn at Vicksburg National Cemetery, situated at the north end of the park near the Mississippi River, cover the graves of 17,000 Union soldiers. The levels step down to the U.S.S. *Cairo* Museum, where the remains of a Union ironclad are on display.

Ironclads were a fearsome sight on the river. Armed with an array of cannons that poked out through two-and-a-half-inch-thick armor sheathing, these steam-powered warships were capable of absorbing barrages of land-based cannon fire with barely a shudder. But the ironclads were not without their faults. Their undersides could not be armored or they would lose their buoyancy, a weakness that appeared minor until five months before the siege of Vicksburg. That December of 1862 the *Cairo* was plying the silty waters of the Yazoo River, just north of its confluence with the Mississippi at Vicksburg, clearing the channel of mines. Suddenly two explosions from an electrically detonated mine tore at her wooden belly, and the *Cairo* sank to the bottom of the river. Only her smokestacks appeared above the surface. It was a historic kill: never before

had a vessel been sunk in this way. The *Cairo* remained submerged in its watery grave for 102 years until it was salvaged in 1964. Since then it has been partially reconstructed and is now on display outside the museum. Inside, artifacts that were rescued from the ironclad are on display, including the ship's engines, boilers, and paddlewheel, and such personal possessions of the crew as coffeepots, pistols, and mess gear.

VICKSBURG CAMPAIGN

Considering the intensity of the 1862–63 campaign for Vicksburg, it is remarkable that anything at all was left to posterity. By the time the Gibraltar of the Confederacy came under siege in May of 1863, west-central Mississippi had suffered numerous battles, including those that took place at Port Gibson, Raymond, Jackson, Champion's Hill, and Big Black River.

General John Clifford Pemberton, commander of the Southern forces defending the Mississippi, had buttressed the town well with earthworks that augmented the terrain's natural severity. Mounds in a variety of shapes—redoubts, redans, lunettes, and parapets—were connected by an extensive maze of trenches and rifle pits that lined the eastern approaches to the town.

The Union had sent amphibious forces on a series of assaults that made no dent in this hilltop bulwark. In the fall of 1862 Grant marched his army toward the town from the north but was foiled by

Confederate cavalry raids on his supply lines. Grant cut a new course for the Mississippi, digging a canal that bypassed the hairpin bend at Vicksburg so that ships on the river could avoid the Confederate batteries on the bluffs. But the river failed to flow into the new course, and Grant realized that Vicksburg would have to be neutralized by a direct assault.

Grant spent much of that winter assembling an army of 35,000 men at Milliken's Bend, located 20 miles upriver from Vicksburg. On March 31, 1863, he mobilized 17,000 of his troops and headed down the western side of the Mississippi into Confederate territory at Bruinsburg, well below Vicksburg. In the meantime his remaining forces harassed key Confederate positions as a diversionary tactic.

Once across the Mississippi River, Grant routed Pemberton's stubborn but outnumbered forces at Port Gibson. But instead of marching directly on to Vicksburg, he sent his army in a northeasterly

MARTIAL TRIBUTE
The U.S. Navy Monument, left, proudly stands as a tribute to the Union navy campaign to reopen the Mississippi River. Statues of the four fleet commanders—Admirals David D. Porter and David G. Farragut and Flag Officers Andrew H. Foote and Charles H. Davis— surround the base of the 202-foot obelisk. The heavy naval cannons in the foreground mark the site of Battery Selfridge, which was named after Thomas O. Selfridge Jr., commander of the U.S.S. Cairo.

direction to sever the vital rail line that linked Vicksburg with the state capital at Jackson.

At that point Grant's troops were joined by men under the command of Gen. William T. Sherman and now stood at nearly 45,000 strong. Having learned that the Confederates had dispatched reinforcements to Jackson, Grant decided to take that city before going to Vicksburg. He knew that if he ignored Jackson, he would risk being trapped between two Southern armies.

There was but token Confederate opposition at Jackson. Grant celebrated the Union victory in the city's finest hotel and set out for Vicksburg. It was left to General Sherman to lay waste to Jackson's railroads and manufacturing facilities and to torch all Confederate government property.

General Pemberton had moved his troops east and now engaged Grant at two strategic points, Champion's Hill and the Big Black River. But his positions were steadily pushed back to the refuge of Vicksburg, where other rebel soldiers had gathered after being scattered by Union forces.

Grant wanted to crush Pemberton's army before it reached Vicksburg. When this proved impossible, he ordered a hasty assault on the Confederate lines, which took place on May 19 at Stockade Redan, an earthen fort that guarded the Graveyard Road to Vicksburg. Grant believed that the rebels were exhausted, disorganized, and could be quickly overrun; instead they rebuffed the assault. Visitors can drive and then climb to the top of the redan where Southern soldiers served notice: Vicksburg would not go down easily.

Three days later Union troops attacked along a three-mile front. Slowed by steep ravines, felled logs, and thick underbrush, the Union assault soon withered beneath the fire of the firmly entrenched Confederate soldiers. Grant suffered heavy losses in his first two attempts and changed his tactics. He established a Union line that was a mirror image of

UNION PRIDE
The equestrian statue of Gen. Ulysses S. Grant, below, by American sculptor Frederick C. Hibbard, was erected in 1918 on the site of the Union army headquarters during the siege.

the Confederate line, built his own earthworks and zigzag trenches, reinforced his artillery positions, and settled in for a long siege.

At the beginning of the battle the two armies were separated by 300 to 600 yards, but the distance between them shrank to as little as 50 feet and rebel resistance weakened as the siege wore on. At times the positions were so close that during lulls in the fighting, opposing soldiers exchanged jokes, enquired about fallen or captured comrades, or traded tobacco and coffee.

Night and day, Union gunboats lobbed shells from the river, and Grant's artillery pounded the besieged town without mercy. While Confederate soldiers stubbornly defended their line, civilians fled to the refuge of hillside caves, taking with them their slaves, furniture, and other personal belongings. One child, born in a cave during the assault, was christened William Siege Green.

Water and medical supplies ran short and mule meat became the food of survival in Vicksburg as the Yankee soldiers tightened the noose, wearing away at the clay forts with explosives and digging their trenches ever closer to the enemy.

On July 3 Pemberton took stock: half of his soldiers were dead, wounded, or sick. He sued for a truce, but steadfastly refused to accept Grant's demands for an unconditional surrender. "You will bury many more of your men before you enter Vicksburg," he warned Grant.

The terms, finally agreed upon by both sides, granted parole for Confederate soldiers and permitted officers to retain their sidearms and mounts. On July 4—47 days after the devastating siege had begun—Federal troops marched into Vicksburg, or what was left of the city.

HISTORIC BUILDINGS

Many of Vicksburg's buildings were damaged or destroyed in the bombardment. One of the surviving structures, Shirley House, is the only wartime building within the military park. Situated a mile or so from the visitor center, the restored "white house," as it was called by Union soldiers, was occupied in May 1863, by Adeline Shirley, her 14-year-old son, and several servants. When the Union army arrived outside Vicksburg, Shirley and the others in the house were caught for three days in a crossfire during which, according to Shirley, "bullets came thick and fast, shells hissed and screamed through the air, cannon roared. . . ." Terrified, they huddled together in a chimney before they were rescued.

The Old Court House, which was built by slaves in 1858, stands on Cherry Street atop a high hill. The building was a favorite target of the Union artillery until captured Union soldiers began to be quartered in the Court House. The Confederate strategy may have saved the building. It is now a Registered National Landmark and museum, commemorating the site where the flag of the United States was raised—and the Confederate flag lowered—after the surrender.

About a dozen of Vicksburg's historic homes are open for tours and a few structures of antebellum vintage still bear the wounds of the war. A cannonball is embedded in the parlor wall of Cedar Grove, an imposing Greek Revival mansion that overlooks the Mississippi and is surrounded by four acres of gardens, fountains, and gazebos. At the McRaven Home on Harrison Street, a live shell from Union artillery was not removed until the 1950's. And the three-story Duff Green Mansion on

UNKNOWN BUT NOT FORGOTTEN
Verses of Theodore O'Hara's 1862 poem "The Bivouac of the Dead" are inscribed on markers along the road through the Vicksburg National Cemetery, above. The cemetery is the final resting place of about 18,000 soldiers; more than 13,000 of them are unidentified.

First East Street was used as a hospital during the conflict. Captured Union wounded were housed on the roof to safeguard the injured Confederate soldiers being treated in the basement.

INTREPID DIARIST Balfour House on Crawford Street, a designated Mississippi landmark, was once the stately home of Emma Balfour, a citizen of Vicksburg who left a detailed account in her diary of the effect the siege had on the city. A center of social activity, the house was the scene of the Confederate Christmas Ball on December 24, 1862, that was broken up by the news that Federal gunboats were churning upriver toward the city.

While many of the 4,500 residents sought refuge from the bombardment in caves they had dug into nearby hills and bluffs, Balfour and her husband, a physician, rode out the onslaught in their home. "I have stayed at home every night except two," wrote Balfour. "I could not stand the mosquitoes and the crowd in the caves. Most people live in them for there is no safety anywhere else; indeed there is no safety there."

TRUE AIM
The bronze figure of a Union cavalryman, right, takes aim from the base of the Wisconsin Monument. The monument bears the names of the 9,059 Wisconsin soldiers who served in the Vicksburg campaign.

HALF-MOON DEFENSE
An earth-and-log fortification, below, once arced for more than eight miles in a protective semicircle around Vicksburg. The city's defenses included 172 big guns, manned by a garrison of 30,000 men.

She wrote about the fighting: "At 12 o'clock the guns all along the lines opened and the parrot shells flew as thick as hail around us! . . . Oh! It is dreadful. After I went to lie down while the Dr. watched every shell from the machines as they came rushing down like some infernal demon. . . . They come gradually making their way higher and higher . . . then with a rush and whiz they come down furiously, their own weight added to the impetus given by the powder. Then look out, for if they explode before reaching the ground . . . the pieces fly in all directions—the very least of which will kill one and most of them of sufficient weight to tear through a house from top to bottom!"

When the fierce bombardment was called to a halt, Federal troops entered the ruined town. Tearful rebels stacked their guns and awaited the humiliation of a Yankee celebration. Instead, the conquering army gave them food and clothing.

One division even cheered the Confederates for their courageous defense of the town.

Five days later, the South lost Port Hudson, their last stronghold on the Mississippi, and the river finally belonged to the Union. The Confederacy was cut in two and the outcome of the war was a virtual certainty. Grant went on to command the entire Union army in a victorious battle with Gen. Robert E. Lee near Richmond, Virginia.

The battle to win control over Vicksburg and its strategic position on the river may have been the decisive engagement of the Civil War. In all, more than 100,000 soldiers gathered and fought in Vicksburg's Walnut Hills. Nearly 15,000 soldiers were killed or wounded and another 5,000 were reported missing in action. It was a battle of varied and complex military actions, involving amphibious assaults, a long siege, and skillful troop movements that military scholars are still studying today. In his analysis of the Civil War, British military expert J. F. C. Fuller concluded that "Vicksburg, not Gettysburg, was the crisis of the Confederacy."

RUNNING THE BLOCKADE
A Currier & Ives lithograph depicts the Union fleet under Admiral Porter running the Confederate batteries at Vicksburg on April 16, 1863. With Porter's flagship, Benton, in the lead, the fleet lost only one transport, Henry Clay, which was set on fire and sunk.

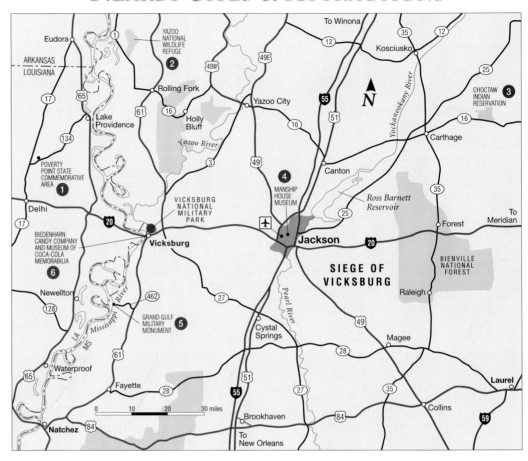

The design of the Manship House, below, was most likely based on a plan in a 19th-century sourcebook for builders titled The Architecture of Country Homes *by A. J. Downing.*

1 POVERTY POINT STATE COMMEMORATIVE AREA, LOUISIANA

This 400-acre park contains 3,000-year-old man-made earth ridges, a crematory mound, a large bird effigy, and a museum. The semicircular ridges are believed to be the foundations of a Native American village that thrived from 1800 to 500 B.C. and was home to about 5,000 people. The ridges, which scientists estimate were once as many as 10 feet high, have eroded to 4 feet in height. Four other mounds and an earthwork effigy of a bird, known as the Poverty Point Mound, are located outside the ridge formations. The bird effigy measures 700- by 800-feet at its base and is 72 feet high. The museum presents a video on the history of the village and its excavation and displays more than 1,000 artifacts. On exhibit are spear points, stone figures, blades, darts, and beads. Two hiking trails take visitors through the area. Although the site was discovered in 1872, its significance was not appreciated until 1953, when it was first viewed from the air. Located 15 miles north of Delhi off Hwy. 134.

2 YAZOO NATIONAL WILDLIFE REFUGE, MISSISSIPPI

This 12,471-acre refuge is a nesting site for wood ducks and the temporary habitat for about 250,000 migratory waterfowl. The bottomland hardwood, agricultural cropland, and wetland vegetation attract approximately 30,000 snow geese and white-fronted geese, great egrets and snowy egrets, bald and golden eagles, 25,000 blue and great herons, swans, and 12 species of ducks, including 10,000 wood ducks that are born in the refuge each spring. Other nesting birds found here include northern orioles, red-headed woodpeckers, and screech, barred, and great horned owls. White ibis find shelter in the willows and buttonbush beside Alligator Pond, which they share with alligators. Other wildlife in the refuge includes coyotes, beavers, white-tailed deer, cottontail rabbits, minks, opossums, raccoons, and bobcats. Five miles of hiking trails and a road wind through the refuge. Located 18 miles north of Rolling Fork off Hwy. 1.

3 CHOCTAW INDIAN RESERVATION, MISSISSIPPI

The reservation hosts the annual Choctaw Fair during the second week of July, which provides visitors with an opportunity to learn about Choctaw history and culture. There are displays of arts and crafts, dancing, and a stickball tournament, which many people consider to be the highlight of the fair. Stickball, believed to be the oldest sport in North America, is related to the game of lacrosse. A museum describes the history of the Choctaw people. The Indians who live on the reservation are the descendants of the 8,000 Choctaw who remained in Mississippi in 1830, when many of their tribe were forcibly moved to Indian Territory in present-day Oklahoma. Located east of Carthage on Hwy. 16.

4 MANSHIP HOUSE MUSEUM, MISSISSIPPI

The home of Charles Henry Manship, a former mayor of Jackson, has been restored to its 1888 appearance and is a rare example of Gothic Revival architecture in the South. The exterior is painted in the cream and olive shades of the original house. The sitting room, parlor, dining room, and three bedrooms feature period furnishings. Manship was a decorative painter, and special faux painting techniques have been used on the walls and ceilings: the baseboards are painted to resemble slate, and the pine mantels to look like marble. Some of the wallpaper imitates oak and mahogany grains. For the restoration, details of the interior were extracted from personal letters, old newspaper articles, photographs, and family recollections. Located at 420 East Fortification St. in Jackson.

5 GRAND GULF MILITARY MONUMENT, MISSISSIPPI

This park contains 19th-century buildings, restored Confederate army forts, and a museum. In the early to mid-19th century, Grand Gulf was an important river port for shipping cotton. In the 1840's and 1850's, a series of disasters struck Grand Gulf, including a fire, a tornado, and an epidemic of yellow fever. Union general Grant wanted to use Grand Gulf as the staging ground for the invasion of Vicksburg. In 1863 Grant ordered seven gunboats on the Mississippi River to fire on the Confederate forts, rifle pits, and gun emplacements in Grand Gulf before sending in a force of 25,000. The troops never landed in Grand Gulf, but the city was devastated by the bombardment. In the late 1950's, buildings that represented Mississippi's diverse architectural styles were moved to Grand Gulf and a carriage house and a mill house were rebuilt at the site. The Confederate forts, rifle pits, and gun emplacements were restored, and a museum opened that displays Native American, pioneer, and Civil War artifacts and memorabilia. Located seven miles northwest of Port Gibson on Hwy. 462.

6 BIEDENHARN CANDY COMPANY AND MUSEUM OF COCA-COLA MEMORABILIA, MISSISSIPPI

Housed in a restored 1890 candy store, this museum recounts the history of Coca-Cola through displays of advertising, memorabilia, and the equipment used in bottling. This popular beverage, named for its main ingredients—the coca leaf and the kola nut—was once available only at soda fountains. In 1894 Joseph Biedenharn became the first person to bottle Coca-Cola so that his rural customers could enjoy the drink at home. In the process, the candy store owner became the first franchise bottler. His combination candy store and office was restored in 1979 with the help of old insurance maps and photographs. It is outfitted with period furnishings. Located at 1107 Washington St. in Vicksburg.

A scale model of the ridges at the Poverty Point State Commemorative Area, above, is on display outside its visitor center.

Joseph A. Biedenharn, the owner of a candy store, shown below, was the first person to bottle Coca-Cola.

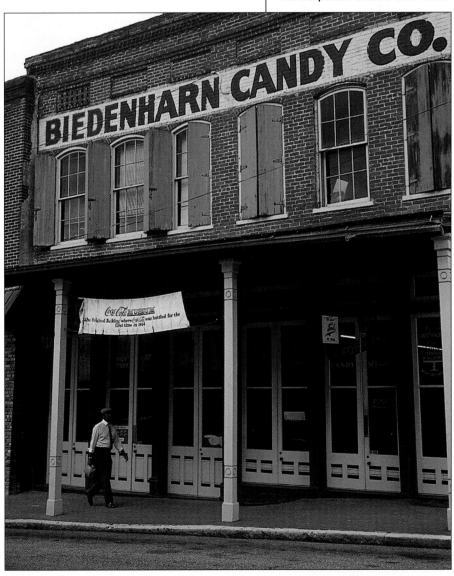

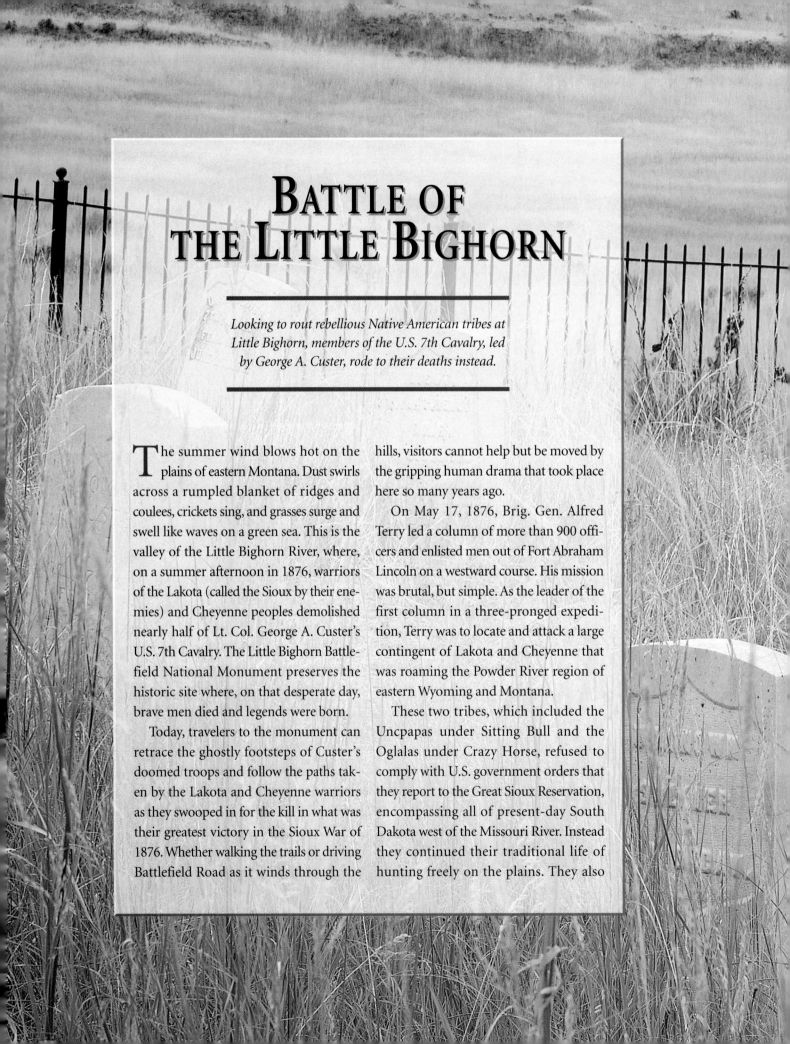

BATTLE OF THE LITTLE BIGHORN

Looking to rout rebellious Native American tribes at Little Bighorn, members of the U.S. 7th Cavalry, led by George A. Custer, rode to their deaths instead.

The summer wind blows hot on the plains of eastern Montana. Dust swirls across a rumpled blanket of ridges and coulees, crickets sing, and grasses surge and swell like waves on a green sea. This is the valley of the Little Bighorn River, where, on a summer afternoon in 1876, warriors of the Lakota (called the Sioux by their enemies) and Cheyenne peoples demolished nearly half of Lt. Col. George A. Custer's U.S. 7th Cavalry. The Little Bighorn Battlefield National Monument preserves the historic site where, on that desperate day, brave men died and legends were born.

Today, travelers to the monument can retrace the ghostly footsteps of Custer's doomed troops and follow the paths taken by the Lakota and Cheyenne warriors as they swooped in for the kill in what was their greatest victory in the Sioux War of 1876. Whether walking the trails or driving Battlefield Road as it winds through the hills, visitors cannot help but be moved by the gripping human drama that took place here so many years ago.

On May 17, 1876, Brig. Gen. Alfred Terry led a column of more than 900 officers and enlisted men out of Fort Abraham Lincoln on a westward course. His mission was brutal, but simple. As the leader of the first column in a three-pronged expedition, Terry was to locate and attack a large contingent of Lakota and Cheyenne that was roaming the Powder River region of eastern Wyoming and Montana.

These two tribes, which included the Uncpapas under Sitting Bull and the Oglalas under Crazy Horse, refused to comply with U.S. government orders that they report to the Great Sioux Reservation, encompassing all of present-day South Dakota west of the Missouri River. Instead they continued their traditional life of hunting freely on the plains. They also

The once frenzied battlefield in the Little Bighorn Valley, above, is silent now. Seen from Weir Point, this site was occupied in 1876 by a huge Native American encampment that stretched for approximately two miles.

TRIBUTE TO THE FALLEN
Overleaf: Prairie grass grows among the headstones on Last Stand Hill. The 42 markers at the gravesite include those of George Custer and his brothers Tom and Boston. Custer's remains were moved to his alma mater, West Point, in 1877.

launched raids on mining camps and white settlements that encroached on their sacred lands, setting a dangerous example, according to most whites, for the disgruntled Native Americans who had been removed to reservations. To reassert their authority, U.S. government officials decided to drive the renegade Lakota and Cheyenne onto reservations—or wipe them out.

TIGHTENING THE NOOSE

In the spring of 1876 small bands of holdout Lakota and Cheyenne were under constant threat of attack from the army. Seeking protection, they migrated toward the secret encampment of the charismatic Lakota chief Sitting Bull, who called for a meeting to discuss the reservation issue. By late June the village numbered some 7,000 members, including 2,000 warriors.

Upon receiving intelligence reports that the camp was located in the vicinity of the Little Bighorn River, Terry devised a lethal battle plan. The 7th

Cavalry, led by the flamboyant Custer, was to launch a mounted attack against the Lakota encampment. Any villagers who escaped Custer's ruthless charge would be scooped up by a column of troops led by Col. John Gibbon in the north.

On June 22 Custer headed off with 632 cavalry troops. Gibbon shouted after him, "Now Custer, don't be greedy, but wait for us." Ever confident, Custer called back with a wave and a smile, "No, I won't." Pushing ahead furiously, he and his troops traveled 73 miles in three days. On the night of June 24 Custer's Crow scouts found signs of a massive concentration of Lakota and Cheyenne just ahead of their campsite. The regiment saddled up immediately and rode through the night in hot pursuit. Custer's plan was to rest on the 25th and raid the village at dawn on the 26th.

When he met with his scouts the next morning, Custer was shown a large cloud of dust some 12 miles distant—a telltale sign that Native Americans and a huge herd of ponies had gathered. The guides also warned Custer that they had spotted enemy scouts and urged caution in the face of what they judged to be an overwhelming foe.

But Custer's life was not about prudence; it was about bravado. During the Civil War he had risen from last in his class at West Point to brevet general in the Union Army by leading daredevil cavalry charges into Confederate lines at Gettysburg, Winchester, and Sailor's Creek. His winning mixture of skill, passion, and luck had made him, by 1876, America's most famous Indian-fighter. Although commanding officers and subordinates often doubted Custer's judgment and disagreed with his tactics, none could deny his success. Now, that success was in jeopardy. Before his regiment was discovered, and the villagers could disperse, he ordered an attack.

Custer divided his regiment into three battalions. Major Marcus Reno, with three companies and 140 men, was to lead a charge into the village from the south. Captain Frederick Benteen and his three companies were sent to survey the territory to the southwest, where the ponies and noncombatants were likely to hide. Custer himself would lead five companies in support of Reno's charge. Shortly after noon the forces divided. Three hours later Reno's men trotted down the North Fork, forded the Little Bighorn, and galloped to the village two and a half miles away.

Visitors can walk through the site where Reno launched his attack. Here, Indian children were splashing in a bend of the Little Bighorn, and women were picking wild turnips in the valley, when suddenly dust rose from the ground to the south. A boy rider named Lone Dog galloped into the village yelling that the cavalry was on his heels. Almost

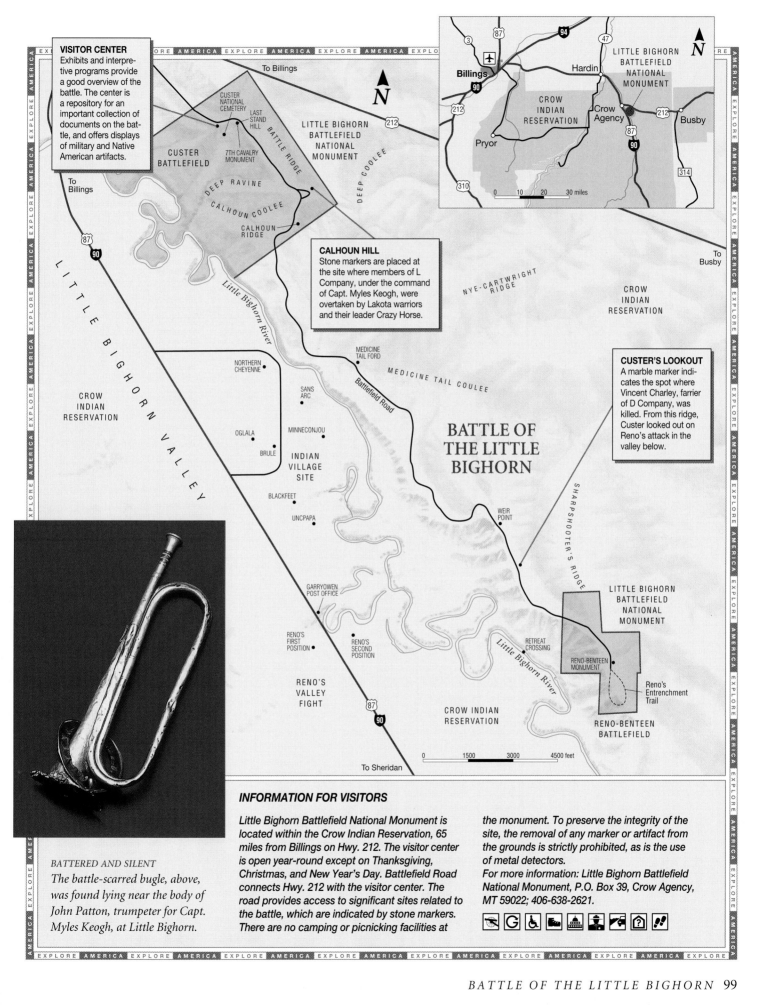

VISITOR CENTER
Exhibits and interpretive programs provide a good overview of the battle. The center is a repository for an important collection of documents on the battle, and offers displays of military and Native American artifacts.

To Billings

CUSTER NATIONAL CEMETERY

LAST STAND HILL

CUSTER BATTLEFIELD

7TH CAVALRY MONUMENT

BATTLE RIDGE

DEEP RAVINE

CALHOUN COOLEE

CALHOUN RIDGE

To Billings

LITTLE BIGHORN BATTLEFIELD NATIONAL MONUMENT

DEEP COOLEE

To Billings

Little Bighorn River

CALHOUN HILL
Stone markers are placed at the site where members of L Company, under the command of Capt. Myles Keogh, were overtaken by Lakota warriors and their leader Crazy Horse.

NYE-CARTWRIGHT RIDGE

CROW INDIAN RESERVATION

To Busby

Billings
Hardin
LITTLE BIGHORN BATTLEFIELD NATIONAL MONUMENT
CROW INDIAN RESERVATION
Crow Agency
Busby
Pryor

0 10 20 30 miles

N

LITTLE BIGHORN VALLEY

CROW INDIAN RESERVATION

NORTHERN CHEYENNE

SANS ARC

OGLALA

MINNECONJOU

BRULE

INDIAN VILLAGE SITE

BLACKFEET

UNCPAPA

MEDICINE TAIL FORD

Battlefield Road

MEDICINE TAIL COULEE

BATTLE OF THE LITTLE BIGHORN

WEIR POINT

SHARPSHOOTER'S RIDGE

CUSTER'S LOOKOUT
A marble marker indicates the spot where Vincent Charley, farrier of D Company, was killed. From this ridge, Custer looked out on Reno's attack in the valley below.

LITTLE BIGHORN BATTLEFIELD NATIONAL MONUMENT

GARRYOWEN POST OFFICE

RENO'S FIRST POSITION

RENO'S SECOND POSITION

RENO'S VALLEY FIGHT

Little Bighorn River

RETREAT CROSSING

RENO-BENTEEN MONUMENT

Reno's Entrenchment Trail

CROW INDIAN RESERVATION

RENO-BENTEEN BATTLEFIELD

0 1500 3000 4500 feet

To Sheridan

N

BATTERED AND SILENT
The battle-scarred bugle, above, was found lying near the body of John Patton, trumpeter for Capt. Myles Keogh, at Little Bighorn.

INFORMATION FOR VISITORS

Little Bighorn Battlefield National Monument is located within the Crow Indian Reservation, 65 miles from Billings on Hwy. 212. The visitor center is open year-round except on Thanksgiving, Christmas, and New Year's Day. Battlefield Road connects Hwy. 212 with the visitor center. The road provides access to significant sites related to the battle, which are indicated by stone markers. There are no camping or picnicking facilities at

the monument. To preserve the integrity of the site, the removal of any marker or artifact from the grounds is strictly prohibited, as is the use of metal detectors.
For more information: Little Bighorn Battlefield National Monument, P.O. Box 39, Crow Agency, MT 59022; 406-638-2621.

MONUMENT TO BRAVERY
The Reno-Benteen Monument, right, marks the spot where Major Reno and Captain Benteen rallied their decimated troops to stave off an assault by Lakota and Cheyenne warriors.

immediately Reno and his troops charged into view. For the Uncpapas, whose village lay directly in Reno's path, there was little time to escape. As Reno's first volley tore into the tepees, the warriors grabbed the weapons at hand—flintlock muskets, repeating rifles, hatchets, clubs, bows and arrows—and ran out to meet the charge.

Older men, including Sitting Bull, helped escort their mothers, wives, and children to safety in the small gullies northwest of the village before joining the fray. As the Uncpapa war chief Gall left to do battle, bullets ripped into his lodge, killing his two wives and three daughters. "It made my heart bad," he later said. Gall took no prisoners this day.

The warriors mounted a fierce resistance, blunting Reno's initial charge from the south. The soldiers dismounted and quickly formed a skirmish line, firing into the village. But the swarming Lakota warriors outflanked the line and forced Reno and his men to withdraw to a more secure position in the woods to the east. At this point in the battle, on the verge of being overwhelmed, Reno may have recalled Custer's last words to him: "You will be supported by the whole outfit," Custer had vowed before he led five companies up onto the ridge tops overlooking the valley to the east, a route now traced by Battlefield Road.

But the support never came. Custer's strategy went with him to the grave. Archeological evidence and the accounts of Lakota and Cheyenne warriors and Reno's men suggest that Custer planned to ride to the far northern end of the village, ford the river, and storm back south to meet Reno, crushing the village in a pincer movement and cutting off the fleeing women and children.

Moving swiftly to the north, Custer divided his forces at upper Medicine Tail Coulee. The left wing, made up of E and F companies under Capt. George Yates and Lt. Algernon Smith and possibly led by Custer, descended to survey a potential ford where the coulee formed a gap in the bluffs. The right wing, consisting of L Company under Lt. James Calhoun, I Company under Capt. Myles Keogh, and C Company under 2nd Lt. Henry Harrington, continued north across Nye-Cartwright Ridge, a long spine of land with a good view of the hills.

Custer's men descended Medicine Tail Coulee and galloped eagerly ahead. Custer joked with them, "Boys, hold your horses. There are plenty of them down there for us all!" He quickly dispatched two messengers with an urgent request, one to the pack train carrying ammunition and another to Benteen: "Come on. Big Village. Be Quick . . . bring packs." By the time Custer finished scouting the crossing, he expected to have nearly 400 men ready to attack. At the ford, Custer was able to observe the size of the village for the first time. Across the river, a group of 30 startled warriors fired back at Custer's troops. The left wing ascended Deep Coulee to rejoin the right wing at Calhoun Hill.

Many historians believe that at this point Custer may have divided his force again, taking the E and F columns ahead to scout another ford and leaving the others to await Benteen on Calhoun Hill. Archeologist Richard Fox suggests Custer's reconnaissance took him beyond today's visitor center to a bow in the river below the national cemetery, the burial place of some 5,000 American soldiers killed in conflicts ranging from the Indian Wars to the Vietnam War. Custer waited for the anticipated reinforcements to strike in force.

FIGHTING FOR THEIR LIVES Farther to the south, beyond Custer's sight, the events had taken a dramatic turn for the worse. Mounting numbers of warriors had driven Reno's cavalry men from the woods and now rode among them, knocking down their horses with war clubs. American Horse, an Oglala, later said it was "like chasing buffalo." In desperation, the panicked soldiers tried in vain to save their lives by urging their horses off a 10-foot embankment and into the swift currents of the river. Several troopers were killed outright, and others were yanked off their horses in midstream by daring young braves. But the warriors did not press their advantage, and remnants of Reno's battered wing reached the relative safety of the opposite bank and scrambled up the steep bluff. The surviving soldiers reassembled at the top of what is now known as Reno Hill, at the southern end of Battlefield Road. In less than an hour some 40 men had been killed.

From the site of the Reno-Benteen Monument on the bluff where the dazed troops gathered, visitors can envision the carnage that took place below. Sharpshooter's Ridge looms in the distance. Atop this hill, hundreds of yards away, a lone warrior picked off three troopers before a furious volley from a half-dozen rifles silenced his gun.

News of the cavalry gathering at Medicine Tail Coulee sped through the village. Warriors—some freed from Reno's valley fight and others, like Crazy Horse, who joined the battle after they prepared themselves spiritually—crossed the river and slipped into ravines to the east. Their numbers were so great, recalled the Cheyenne Two Moons, that they looked like "ants rushing out of an anthill."

To attack Keogh's detachment, the group of warriors crossed over the ridge and crept through the sage, picking off soldiers with rifles and lethal volleys of arrows. Many of these troopers were raw recruits, inexperienced in the unconventional tactics of the Indians. Nonetheless, they held the warriors at bay with their single-shot Springfield carbines. When a large number of Lakota and Cheyenne gathered in Calhoun Coulee, C Company charged down the slope toward Calhoun Ridge and dismounted to form a skirmish line. They never fired a shot.

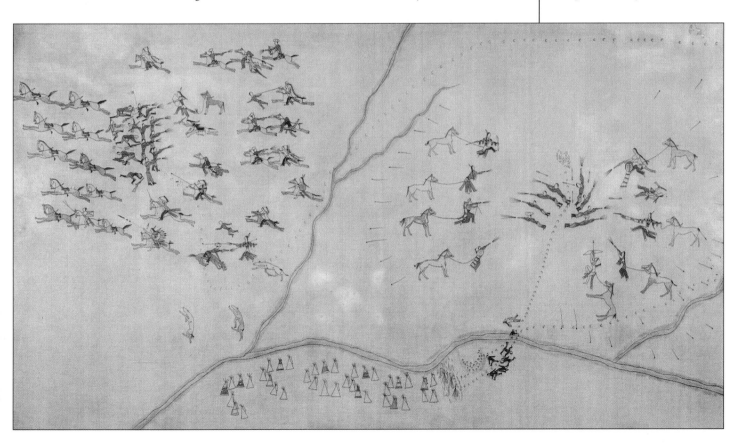

ARTIST'S RENDERING

Lt. Col. George A. Custer takes center stage in Custer's Last Stand, below, as he and soldiers of the E and F companies are swarmed by warriors. The huge canvas was painted by Edgar S. Paxson in 1899, and is on display in the Buffalo Bill Historical Center in Cody, Wyoming. Like other paintings of the battle, Paxson's includes historical inaccuracies, not the least of which is that some historians believe Custer may already have been dead at this point in the melee.

Swooping in on horseback, Cheyenne warriors under Lame White Man overran the line, chasing C Company back up the hill in terror. In all, some 40 soldiers were killed.

Chiefs Gall and Runs the Enemy led Lakota horsemen in a charge against another skirmish line from the south. When hand-to-hand combat broke out, the desperate soldiers cast aside their single-shot carbines as useless, relying instead on their Colt .45 revolvers. Even these proved ineffective in the dusty fighting that ensued.

Noting a weakness in the right wing, Crazy Horse crashed his mount directly through the line, dividing the besieged troops into two smaller groups and shattering the last remnant of military discipline. Keogh's I Company, engulfed in panic, shot wildly. As they fought their way toward the intact companies of the left wing, more than 80 soldiers were killed by rampaging warriors. Today their grave markers—placed where each man fell—line

Battlefield Road on the crest of Calhoun Ridge, reminding visitors of the troops' last hopeless moments as warriors closed in on them.

The left wing occupied a small rise called Last Stand Hill. When the survivors of the right wing staggered over the rise, there on the exposed slope stood Custer and a mere 102 men. Hundreds of warriors picked them off from behind the tall grass below. The troopers took cover as well as they could, some lying flat on their bellies, others crouching behind fallen horses. But there was nowhere to hide. The Lakota came from the south and the Cheyenne from the north. Like the doomed C Company before it, E Company now tried futilely to repel the surging waves of warriors. About 45 soldiers rushed the Lakota along the ridge to the south, but heavy fire instantly mowed down some 40 of them. A few made it into Deep Ravine.

Roughly 40 soldiers remained on Last Stand Hill. Shooting their horses and using them for cover,